£E25.00

# CENTERED RIDING

# CENTERED RIDING

## by Sally Swift

*Photography by Mike Noble*
*Drawings by Jean MacFarland*

**A Trafalgar Square Farm Book**
David & Charles Inc.
North Pomfret, Vermont

ST. MARTIN'S PRESS
NEW YORK

Cover photo: Anne Hutchins on *Argraff Nwyfus Y Penrhyn* (Welsh Cob), taken at Huntington Farm, South Strafford, Vermont.

A Trafalgar Square Farm Book
David & Charles Inc.
North Pomfret, Vermont 05053

Library of Congress Cataloging in Publication Data

Swift, Sally, 1913-
    Centered riding.

    1. Horsemanship.  I. Title.
SF309.S995   1985        798.2'3        84-22351
ISBN 0-312-12734-0


33  32  31  30  29  28

**Book design by Mark Gabor**

# Contents

# Acknowledgments

With appreciation and thanks to the people who have helped this book come to fulfillment: To Mabel Elsworth Todd, who taught me so much about my body, who made it possible for me to ride during much of my life, and who instilled in me my first knowledge of centering. To Jean Gibson for furthering that knowledge. And most specially to Peter Payne, who in the last four years has patiently rebuilt my body through the Alexander Technique so that I could continue to work. He has in many ways enriched the scope of my teaching and has also given invaluable advice on the technical drawings in this book.

To Doris Eddy for giving me the first inklings of the subtle feel and beauty of the movement of free, soft horses. To Tom Poulin for opening a door that might never have been opened had he not invited me to be a guest-observer of fine, high-level horses. To Priscilla Hergersheimer for the days and hours I sat at her ringside, absorbing the knowledge and teaching of Major Hans Wikne and Walter Christenson, both of whom I also thank. To Denny Emerson for his steady support, his big push for me to "write it down," and finally for writing the Foreword. To Essie and Read Perkins for letting me use Huntington Farm as a laboratory to experiment with my ideas. And again to Denny, and his wife, May, of Tamarack Hill Farm, and to Jill and Charles Bronson of Zuleika Farm, where most of the photographs were taken. And to the countless friends who have been my willing and enthusiastic guinea pigs over the years.

To Jean MacFarland for her skillful drawings and her patience when asked to have them slightly changed many times over. To Mike Noble for his perseverance and enthusiasm through the hours of taking and processing some 2600 photographs. To my cousin Jane Ashley for being such a stalwart and patient subject for most of these pictures. And to Tara and Gregory Prince.

To Huntly Hashagen, who succeeded in deciphering and typing the original manuscript for this book. To Karen McCollom, who worked long and hard to put some order into that confusing mass of material. To Mark Gabor, first for his many hours that went into the early editing, and later for designing the book so elegantly.

Lastly, and most importantly, to Caroline Robbins for actually making this book possible through her untold hours of precise editing, as well as all the rest of the details involved in the total publishing of this book.

*Dedicated to my sister*
**Agnes Swift**
*and to my friend*
**Rosa Tyson**
*who housed, nurtured, and encouraged me over many years*

# Foreword

Most of us have been thoroughly imbued with the puritan work ethic, which postulates that the attainment of success is directly proportionate to the degree of struggle we expend on it. From the time we enter school we are told to study harder to get better grades, do more push-ups, run more laps to make the football team. "If you don't try, you won't succeed." Then we climb onto a horse, a timid creature of flight, which knows and cares nothing of the work ethic, and we drive him crazy. The very act of trying brings tension and rigidity; the horse responds to our stress with his stress, and the downward spiral begins.

Sally Swift, with quiet wisdom and gentle understanding, asks us to reassess our habitual responses and in so doing alter the way we approach riding and training horses.

To understand the main cause of much of our problems with horses, we need to understand the history of riding. In Europe the tradition of classical riding was usually taught by the military. Raw recruits were placed on schooled horses, often on the lunge line, and then drilled for hours a day for months to attain "good seats." It was survival of the fittest, with lots of dropouts. The recruit had to overcome the physical pain of the moving horse and the emotional pain of the screaming instructor. If he adjusted his posture incorrectly to alleviate the physical stress, he got the brunt of verbal correction. Over months, little by little, the recruit who stayed with the program learned to ride. He may not have known, anatomically, what his body did to accommodate itself to the horse's moving body, but he became a part of that motion. As well as that system works—and it does work, brilliantly—it requires hundreds of hours of time, numerous horses, and constant access to a good instructor. Today, very few riders can afford the time, horses or instructor.

Sally Swift has bridged the gap in traditional riding instruction with a thorough knowledge of human and equine anatomy and an analytical, but relaxed, approach to the two. If people can understand how they move, how a horse moves, how they interact, postulates Sally, then they can shortcut, through understanding, at least some of the endless hours of blind rote.

This book is in part Sally's response to the many of us who have been helped by her lessons and who have urged her to "Write it down, organize it, create a book!" So she did. I believe that the readers will feel through its pages the same spirit and wisdom, gentleness and common sense that Sally conveys to those of us lucky enough to be her students.

EDWARD E. EMERSON JR.
*President U.S. Combined Training Association*
*Member U.S. Equestrian Team 1974 World Championships and 1976 Olympic Games*

# 1

# Introducing Centered Riding

This book, on the whole, does not teach you how to ride. There are countless excellent books that do just that. What I do here is offer all riders a new approach to riding based on some mental and physical images that I have developed over many years. It is a centered approach, resulting in perfect body balance and an inner awareness of both yourself and your horse.

I would like to emphasize that this is not a book for the dressage enthusiast alone, although many of the techniques discussed apply to that discipline. It is a book for all riders and the techniques discussed apply equally to jumpers, hunters, or people who like to hack. I use the word dressage to mean "training," and this book focuses on the training of both horse and rider for all varieties of equestrian sport. I teach you about a relationship between you and your horse based on a self-awareness that you probably have never realized you had inside you.

If you are a novice or intermediate rider, you will not have learned the subtleties of the horse/rider relationship experienced by expert riders, but these insights, as they come into play, cannot but raise your level of skill and heighten your riding performance. If you are already at an advanced level, you will be able to use these images and exercises to refine your technique and gain that special magic—that something extra—that makes the difference between competence and excellence. Many of the great riders have the gift of natural balance and coordination so that they never have to question *how* to do anything with any part of their body. If they know what they want to do, their body will respond. Because of this innate coordination, they have not needed to know *how* one makes a leg move, or *how* one breathes, or *how* one balances. It just happens. Therefore it is usually difficult for them to explain to the rest of us less-coordinated mortals how to move some particular part of our bodies.

As a child I certainly was not coordinated or balanced. I had to learn the hard way in every step of my riding career. Because I had a back problem, I was specially taught how to deal with my very awkward body. Through my experiences on learning how to control my body, I developed the techniques given in this book. It was my own back that forced me to concentrate so intently on how the body of a rider functions, and what can be done to improve its efficiency.

When I was eight years old I was diagnosed as having a lateral curvature of the spine—technically known as scoliosis. This was probably caused by an unrecognized case of polio. In order to care for and correct my back problem, I worked with Mabel Ellsworth Todd in Boston from the time I was eight years old into my early twenties. Her premise was that with our minds we can control deep, inner muscles that we would not be able to activate by moving just an arm or a leg. She wrote a book called *The Thinking Body*—the title gives some idea of her approach. She taught a lot of anatomy; a skeleton was always hanging nearby, and books were brought out frequently to show how muscles looked and worked. She used a great many images for teaching, such as squatting down and walking like a duck or, when walking upright, dragging an imaginary alligator's tail along the ground. So I grew up surrounded by this teaching of anatomy and images.

By the time I was thirteen years old, I was very overdeveloped on my right side. In order to counter this, Miss Todd made me learn to write with my left hand and give up all sports that required the use of my right hand. She knew, however, that it was important that I enjoy some sort of physical activity; since horses had been my passion for as long as I could remember, she encouraged me to ride. This was excellent therapy because riding uses both sides of the body equally. In order for me to ride, however, Miss Todd sent me to an orthopedist who constructed a corset brace, leather with steel supports, which I used for many years. I took some bad spills in it, too, but never hurt my back.

By developing equal use of my two legs in riding, I strengthened the muscles in my lower body and balanced my uneven muscle tone. Miss Todd's work prevented me from tipping off center by making the spinal curvature compensate itself. The top of my head was above my pelvis and not off to one side, as is the case with many scoliotic people. I was very fortunate because people in my circumstances were often put into full-body casts or had spinal fusions or other unpleasant experiences I was able to avoid. I was given the freedom of many years of enormous happiness on a horse.

After I finished school I taught riding for twelve years, then went into other fields for thirty years. By 1967 my back had deteriorated, though I still did exercises that Miss Todd had taught me years earlier. At this time I was standing tipped to the side and was frequently in pain. In London I met Jean Gibson, who was doing therapy similar to Miss Todd's. I worked with her two weeks a year for three years. During these periods my input was very concentrated. Jean is emphatic that each part of the body be correctly balanced on the parts below and that the joints be used fully. She feels that this allows the other parts of the body to do their jobs without tensions and extra fatigue, and with balance and rhythm. I immediately realized that everything she taught me applied also to riding, and I have used her work to the full in my teaching. Jean Gibson was responsible for bringing me once again to an upright position and rebalancing my body so that most of the time, though I lived in a brace, I was out of pain—healthiest and happiest, as always, when teaching.

Currently I am working with Peter Payne in Brattleboro, Vermont, where I live. Peter has had extensive training in the martial arts and other forms of body control, culminating in a full course of study in the Alexander Technique (a method of reeducating the mind and body toward greater balance and integration, with special reference to posture and movement). This work is not only reestablishing strength and balance in my ever-tending-to-be-wobbly back, but also enlarges my knowledge of techniques as a riding teacher.

When I was in my twenties, I discovered from working with Miss Todd that if I rode from the center of my body, I stayed in better balance and my horse responded better. Jean Gibson later made me tremendously aware again of centered body control and the importance of breathing and balance. Increasingly, I began to realize that there was a great gap in most people's riding knowledge. Even the best riders and instructors, with their innate coordination, were not teaching people how to *handle* their bodies. They were teaching them only what to *do*. We who have struggled with physical disabilities can often teach and explain coordination more easily.

In his book *The Ultimate Athlete*, George Leonard searches for the perfect athlete and finds much of what he is looking for in the Oriental martial arts, which are based on centered control. In another book, *The Centered Skier*, Denise McCluggage has developed a method of teaching skiing with centered control that echoes my work almost completely. She, too, had been exposed to the martial arts, having studied t'ai chi ch'uan, the foundation of all the martial arts. I discovered I wasn't teaching anything new, I was just a Johnny-come-lately. I had earlier discovered the importance of control from the center of the body, and the need for awareness, correct breathing, and quietness of the balanced body. Now I am aware that many of these concepts in fact came from the East and are more than two thousand years old.

It is the combination of how your body works, the ability to allow it to function unhampered, and the awareness and use of energies created through you and your horse that makes this approach to riding surprisingly easy and very exciting.

# 2

## Pretend You Are a Horse

Have you ever tried pretending you were a horse? Have you thought what it would feel like to have a rider on your back telling you what to do? Would it be comfortable and enjoyable? Would it be uncomfortable and awkward? If you carry a well-packed knapsack on your back that is also well balanced over your shoulders, it is not an unpleasant feeling. But if it is loosely packed, unbalanced, and not strapped on correctly, it can be very uncomfortable and seem much heavier than it actually is.

There is another way of pretending you are a horse. Get down on your hands and knees, keeping your back level. Move around the floor a bit, being careful not to hump your back or let it sag. It will help to check yourself in a full-length mirror. Then have a friend poke you sharply with two stiff fingers on either side of your spine just at the base of your shoulder blades. What is your reaction to these sharp pokes? *Ouch!* (Fig. 1.) You quickly hollow your back and your head snaps up. Have your friend poke you in different places nearer your pelvis. Each time you will find the same reaction, especially when the pokes are a little farther down. It is not a pleasant exercise.

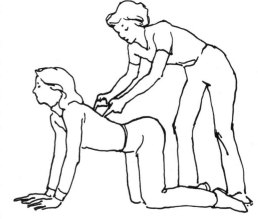

1. *"Ouch!" This is what we sometimes do to our horses.*

Is this the sort of thing we do to our horses when we don't sit to the trot correctly, when we bang the saddle at the canter, when we post to the trot and come down too heavily, or when we mount and land—*thump*—on the horse's back? Your reaction in the exercise was to shrink away from thumps and bumps—to hollow your back and raise your head. How many times have you seen a horse react in just this way? He is unhappy, tense, his back hollowed. His nose is up, his eyes have an inner, frightened look, and his ears are back. He looks tentative, distressed; he switches his tail and moves with short, stiff strides.

A horse will react to more subtle discomfort, too. In the dressage ring you may have watched a rider trying to make the horse round his back, come on the bit, and swing his hind legs under, yet the horse resists all efforts, not wanting to raise and stretch his back—all this because he is uncomfortable under the rider's seat bones, which are unwittingly punishing him.

Now let's change the picture and try another experiment with you on all fours on the floor. Have your friend, instead of poking you rather rudely, play with his or her fingers on your back in a rather pleasant way, working on both sides of the spine at once. (Fig. 2.) Or let your friend caress your back, gently massaging you. It feels wonderful, doesn't it? And what's your reaction? To raise your back, stretch and arch it up like a cat. You could even purr. It is certainly not a sensation that you are going to cringe from, but one that you are going to accept and even enjoy. Wouldn't it be nice to give that kind of pleasure to your horse when you are riding him?

Have you ever seen a horse, resistant and stiff with one rider, respond quite differently to another rider? (Fig. 3.)

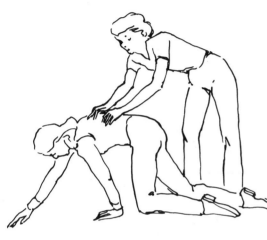

*2. "Oooh . . . Wonderful!" Any horse would like this better.*

*3. Unhappy horse.*

6

This second rider mounts the horse, springing lightly up and settling gently in the saddle. They move off quietly, the rider's body flowing and swinging with the horse's body. The horse strides out freely, head down, ears relaxed, eyes quiet. Gently, the rider picks up the reins and moves the horse on, body balanced, hardly touching the horse's back in the rising trot. (Fig. 4.) Circles become easy. There is no resistance. The horse bends softly. The rider goes on into the sitting trot, then the canter, and still there is no tension because the body is swinging with the horse. The horse is both enjoying his rider and is willing to cooperate and move as he is asked. The horse's strides are supple and open, the rhythm pleasant to watch; impulsions come softly from behind with energy flowing through his body. Under such a rider a horse becomes transformed. Even a horse with actual physical problems will be improved to some degree.

Under the first rider, one has the impression that the horse is saying, "I wish he'd get off my back. I'm frustrated. He gives conflicting aids, and I don't know what he wants; or when I do know what he wants, he doesn't

4. *Happy horse.*

let me do it. He gets in the way and is banging on my back. His inside leg is stiff. If he'd soften it, I'd soften my side, but I'm not going to soften against that iron object. I can't swing my legs when I'm being hit in the back. I'm unhappy. I can't move the way he wants me to."

Conversely, when the second rider mounts, you can almost hear the horse sigh with relief. "Oh, this is so much better," he might be saying. "It's easy to move under this rider because he's totally with me, swinging with me; it even makes *me* swing more. I like working under him. Now I can bring my hind legs under and round my back."

The reasons for the change between the two riders is not only that the second rider uses aids better than the first, though certainly this comes into it. Usually much of the difference lies in *how* those aids are applied. You are taught what to do and when, but seldom how to use your own body when applying these aids. Try as you will, your recalcitrant body won't let you do what you're trying so desperately to do, and your poor horse is left frustrated and confused.

You would like to ride like the second rider—to learn where to sit in the saddle so that you are balanced and positioned correctly. But when the horse moves, the problems begin, and you find yourself stiffening up in an effort to maintain a balanced position. As you continue to struggle for the proper position, it becomes more difficult to remain in balance. You become tense and frustrated.

The tendency is to feel that the horse is partly at fault. Perhaps he is obstinate or badly coordinated and finds it physically difficult to move correctly. This may be part of it, and may have some influence on the way he is going. But usually that's not the whole picture. The horse has been put in a situation where not only is he uncomfortable, but he is also being told to do something at the same time he is being prevented from doing it. (Fig. 5.) How frustrated would you be if somebody gave you a ball and asked you to throw it, but first tied your elbows behind your back? This is the sort of thing we do to our horses.

Some riders do not have to argue with their own bodies, but can spend their time learning what to tell their horses while their bodies do the work easily and automatically.

8

Unfortunately, most people are not this well-coordinated. Under the proper direction, however, they can improve coordination, first learning how their bodies work—for instance, how to move different parts independently from other parts—and then, with an inner consciousness of the correct form and balance, how to merge the whole process together.

The perfect rider cannot immediately produce the finished horse. Just as a human gymnast must spend countless hours developing muscles and coordination, so must the horse go through many hours of carefully planned activity and schooling to develop correctly the muscles and balance needed to carry a rider on his back and produce the preformance that is desired—be it jumping, dressage competition, long-distance trail riding, or just plain hacking.

In the following chapters I'll be showing you many techniques and exercises to help make you a centered rider. There is no set rule about how many repetitions you should do of each exercise. Usually two or three repeats are enough to relieve tension or give you the sensation you are looking for. The type of exercise I recommend does not involve getting fatigued. Rather, it is usually a way of learning to feel a new movement or concept. It is a route to softness that some people find more quickly than others. If any particular exercise doesn't work for you, don't worry—just try a different one.

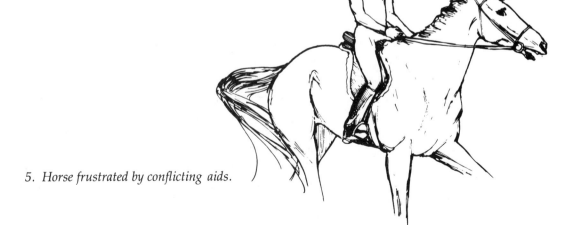

5. *Horse frustrated by conflicting aids.*

# 3

## The Four Basics

*In order to make your horse happy by knowing and controlling your own body better, you must start riding with what I call the Four Basics. These Four Basics are fundamental to all of my teaching. They consist of the correct use of eyes, breathing, centering, and building blocks.*

### *Eyes*

Let's experiment with your eyes. First, halt your horse. While sitting quietly, focus very intently on one thing, perhaps a letter marker or a certain post or object on the edge of the ring. Keep looking intently at the object. Concentrate on its exact outlines, its shape, density, color. Take everything in acutely. This is the use of what I call hard eyes.

Now relax your eyes. Let the object be the general center of your gaze, but look at it with your peripheral vision taking in the largest possible expanse, above and below as well as to the left and right. Be aware of the whole wide world. Sit comfortably with open eyes and have the feeling of going within yourself as your eyes encompass everything that comes into your field of vision. Remember that you are still aiming at the central object. This is what I call soft eyes. The concept will be invoked and practiced throughout this book.

What did you see when you looked with hard eyes? Did you see anything besides the object you were looking at? Not if you really focused. What did you see when you were looking with soft eyes? You probably saw at least half the arena even though your general focus was toward one object. When I teach the use of soft eyes, I start by standing in front of riders and then walk a semicircle around them, asking them to tell me when I disappear from sight. Standing on that spot, I ask them to look at me. Most are very surprised at how far they must turn their heads to find me. Usually I am standing well behind their shoulders before I disappear. What does this mean to a rider? It means simply that your eyes can give you much greater awareness if you allow them.

Try another experiment. While walking your horse without stirrups, shift back and forth between hard eyes and soft eyes. Hard eyes are easy to do if you look at your horse's ears. Soft eyes, with your vision very wide and open, are easy to do if you look above his ears out into space. Which way do you suppose it is easier to feel what your horse's back is doing to your seat? You will quickly find that it is much easier to feel this when using soft eyes. The more area you encompass with your eyes, the more you'll be aware of your seat. Glazing or making your eyes fuzzy is not your objective; that would most likely reduce what you feel with your seat.

From this experiment it becomes clear that soft eyes are much more than just a way of looking. Using soft eyes is like a new philosophy. It is a method of becoming distinctly aware of what is going on around you, beneath you, inside of you. It includes feeling and hearing as well as seeing. You are aware of the whole, not just separate parts. Ponder the implications of this technique, this tool. The two ears of your horse are always in front of you, but so many of the important parts are under and behind you, where you cannot see them.

When I first started teaching the technique of soft eyes, I had an exciting experience with four girls, good riders, all reaching for their Pony Club B-rating. Working in a small arena, these four girls rode for nearly fifteen minutes with soft eyes, each following her own, varied program, with up and down transitions, circles, turns, serpentines, and changes of direction. Not only did they do some superb riding, but during the entire time nobody came near to running into anyone else. Because of the soft eyes, they were constantly aware of where everyone else was and could therefore plan their movements so that each girl worked independently without bothering another.

Another student of mine was Sarah. When her eight-year-old daughter, Brooke, came home from a hack, Brooke was furious with her pony, who had been totally ill-tempered and uncooperative all the way. She was determined to sell the animal and give up riding. Sarah took time to tell Brooke all about the idea of soft eyes. It was like a new kind of game. Then she suggested that Brooke ride her pony to the end of the road and back. Off she went, cantering gaily, then turned and came trotting home all smiles. When Sarah asked Brooke what her body had felt like with soft eyes, Brooke thought a moment, then said excitedly, "Like jelly!" Brooke kept the pony.

Soft eyes have other applications, too. Well-known event rider Denny Emerson uses them in competition. Just before the stadium jumping phase, he takes two or three minutes to sit quietly on his horse, and, going inside himself with eyes very soft, he rides the whole course mentally. Later, during the actual ride, he can then flash back and forth between hard and soft eyes as needed.

*What are the essentials of soft eyes?*

- Ride with wide-open eyes and peripheral awareness.
- Maintain awareness of your entire field of vision.
- Allow yourself to feel sensations from within.

*What are the results of soft eyes?*

- Greater field of vision.
- Increased awareness of your own and your horse's body.
- Fewer tensions.
- Easier and freer forward movement.

## *Breathing*

The second of the Four Basics, correct use of breath, is vitally important and closely related to the other Basics. We will refer to breathing throughout this book, so it is important that you have a good visual and mental image of how the whole breathing process works.

In breathing you must think about your diaphragm—a powerful muscle that goes across the body beneath the rib cage. The front end is just at the bottom of your sternum, or breast bone. (Fig. 6.) The diaphragm is shaped like a dome or mushroom; it cups up into the rib cage. Its root is attached to the front of the lower spine. It is one of the largest muscles in your body. When you inhale, the diaphragm is pulled down, creating a vacuum in the lungs and drawing in air. When you exhale, the muscle relaxes, the diaphragm rises to the resting position, and air is pushed out.

When asked to take a deep breath, many people will expand the rib cage sideways and upward as much as possible, forgetting about the diaphragm. This is an inefficient way to breathe. The diaphragm should be pulled down, and if the rib cage and shoulders are not tense, the ribs will open automatically and the back will spread as a result of the incoming air. If we breathe as nature intended, the lungs are given a chance to fill the large area created by a *somewhat* expanded rib cage. The diaphragm is the major mover, followed by the ribs.

As you walk on your horse, use your imagination and soft eyes and feel that your breath is going down through your body to your belt line and even beyond, into your pelvis. If you can, imagine that it is going down even farther, maybe all the way into your boots. If you feel activity at and below your belt line, you are not actually feeling air, but the motion of the muscles pulling the diaphragm down.

Now put your hand flat across your belly, thumb upon your navel. If you are breathing correctly with your diaphragm, you will feel action under your hand. Now try deliberately breathing only from your chest; you will find

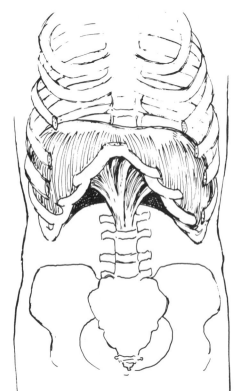

6. *The diaphragm looks like a mushroom. Its root is attached to the lower spine and pulls the diaphragm down to draw breath in and relaxes to let it out.*

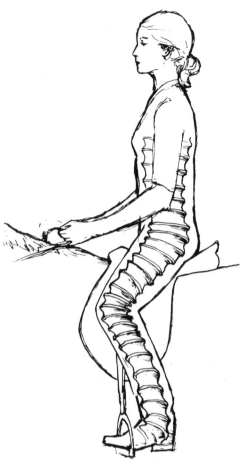

7. *Breathe through your whole body. Imagine that you can breathe all the way down into your feet through an imaginary flexible tube.*

no action under your hand. Then return to the correct, effortless, normal breathing that involves your entire body.

It is easier to work with mental images than to think of specific muscles. Try feeling that the air is going through a big, flexible tube, right down through the center of your body to the bottom. (Fig. 7.) I have one friend who feels that this tube is large, elastic, and blue. You can imagine it any way you wish.

Visualizing that you are breathing to a point below your belt line helps make the diaphragm descend. Then, if you simply *allow* the ribs to expand without force, you will have air intake with less physical tension than if you were to breathe by consciously raising your ribs. Denise Mc-Cluggage has some wonderful breathing images in *The Centered Skier*. She says the difference between breathing with your chest and breathing with your diaphragm is like the difference between balloons and bellows. You have to push hard to blow up a balloon (Fig. 8); you have to make a strenuous effort to suck the air in through your nostrils and spread your chest out all over the place to fill it. Yet this is the way many people breathe. Bellows, however, open easily to let the air rush in and close easily to let it out. (Fig. 9.) So instead of imagining a balloon in your

8. *Breathing only in your chest is like blowing up a balloon. It is hard work.*

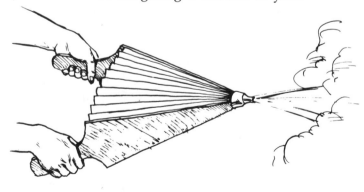

9. *Breathing with a bellows in your lower body is easier and more efficient.*

14

chest, visualize a bellows between your diaphragm and your pelvis and quietly keep it opening and shutting. It will do all the work for you; your nostrils will only be the funnel. The ribs lift and spread softly and automatically, then drop again. Their motion becomes the *result* of breathing, not the cause. Open the bellows, in flows oxygen; close it, out goes carbon dioxide.

Try holding your breath for ten seconds, then breathe normally. Did you feel the tension in your body when your breath was held? And did you feel your body relax when you began to breathe again? When you hold your breath, you build certain tensions in your body to which a horse will react. I discovered this fact many years ago while riding Kim, a hot little horse at Colonel Guirey's, in his covered arena in New York City. He was concentrating on two other riders and I was left happily on my own. My horse never wanted to do a flat walk. He'd always rather jig or go even faster. I was determined to make him do a flat walk around that ring. I tried everything I could think of, including holding my breath. We could get almost around the ring, but at the letter B, Kim always jigged. I remember saying to myself in desperation, "I give up, I just won't do anything." I sat relaxed, breathing normally, and then Kim started walking quietly around the ring and past B time after time, never jigging, as long as I kept breathing. If I changed my breathing pattern, he was off. I tried trotting. Again, if I breathed rhythmically, he would not hurry. Suddenly I was conscious of the Colonel watching me intently as I circled. "What have you done to Kim, Miss Swift?" he asked. Being young, I somehow felt embarrassed. "I'm just breathing, Colonel," I replied.

How would you feel if your horse held his breath? Frightened, most likely. And that's the way he'd feel if you held yours. You can breathe a horse to quietness. You can breathe him past things that scare him. If you hold your breath as you come to that big rock, he'd say, "She's frightened! There must be gremlins there." (Fig. 10.) But if you keep breathing or talking (you can't hold your breath when you are talking), it gives him confidence. Breathing must be done without tension. Allow it to be constant and rhythmical. Holding your breath blocks the suppleness in certain parts of your body. And remember to allow yourself to breathe through your *whole* body.

10. *If you hold your breath,*
*gremlins will jump out at you.*

*What are the essentials of correct breathing?*
- Breathe through your whole body.
- Breathe rhythmically and constantly.
- Allow the bellows to work.

*What are the results of correct breathing?*
- Reduced tension in your body.
- Body becomes less top-heavy.
- Center of gravity becomes lower.
- Horse becomes quieter and more responsive.
- Rider will not tire as easily.

# Centering

The third of the Four Basics is centering. In order to effectively control your body and your horse's, you must be able to find your center. Most of us tend to be top and front oriented. We also fuss too much about details, do a lot of over-organizing, and breathe mostly in our chests. All these characteristics increase our tension, reduce our mobility, raise our center of gravity, make us top-heavy, and reduce our coordination. By centering—lowering our center of control—we can overcome these tendencies.

If you watch someone riding and he looks off balance, jerky, or stiff, it is almost always because the center is wrong. The rider is usually behind his own balance and behind the motion of the horse. If he can get the center correct, the rest will fall into place.

To find your center, simply point a finger at your belly to a spot between your navel and your pubic arch, the front of your pelvis. (Fig. 11.) Deep behind that point, against the front of your spine, lies your center of balance, your center of energy, and your center of control. From the bottom of your diaphragm and rib cage, large muscles stretch to the lower spine. Other muscles connect from there into the pelvis and down to the thighs. These are some of the deepest and strongest muscles in your body. If you were to cut yourself in half at your center, you would find that, because the lower, or lumbar, vertebrae are very thick, the front of your spine is actually in the center of the circle of your body, not at the back, as you might have thought. (Fig. 12.) Down here, deep and close to the lumbar spine, you also have the largest bundle of muscle-controlling nerves in your body. At the site of this large nerve center and the heavy, controlling muscles, is your center.

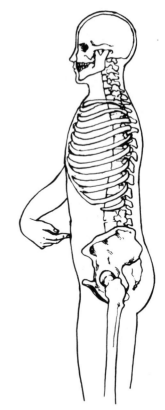

11. *Pointing to your center.*

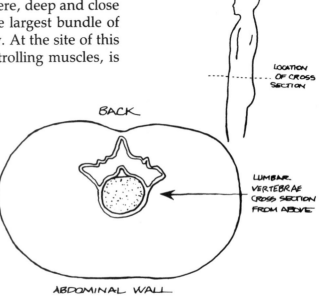

12. *Cross section of your lower body at your center. The spine at this point is so thick that its front is in the center of your body.*

BACK

LOCATION OF CROSS SECTION

LUMBAR VERTEBRAE CROSS SECTION FROM ABOVE

ABDOMINAL WALL

How do you achieve centered control? Use your soft eyes to become aware of your body and organize your breathing. With your diaphragm, let your breathing slide down through your body and you will find yourself breathing to and through your center. For you it may come simply through breathing, or perhaps from images like a great hand at your center, or an internal electric generator sparking energy, or by grabbing a bunch of your shirt below your belt. Allow yourself to be one of those rocking dolls that are heavily weighted at the bottom. (Fig. 13.) You can push the top over as far as you want, but it will always bounce upright again. This is the way your body should feel—so stable and deep at the bottom that the top can do nothing but remain balanced and upright.

If you find a particular image or thought that works for you, hold on to it, because every time you return to that image, you will automatically feel that centered control. Many times I have rescued a circle that was about to turn into a pear by saying quickly to a student, "Center yourself now, and now, and now." You cannot force yourself to do this. If you have difficulty learning how to center yourself, take your time, give your body a chance, don't force it. *Retire* to your center and be quiet. Let your breathing become organized. Breathe to your center.

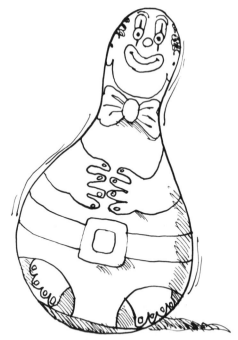

13. *If you imagine that you are a doll weighted at the bottom, you will remain stable.*

### What are the essentials of centering?

- Find your physical center with your hand.
- Use soft eyes.
- Breathe down through your center.
- Allow your awareness to drop to your center.

### What are the results of centering?

- Balance, control, and energy are established.
- Center of gravity is lower.
- Upper body seems lighter, more stable, and easier to handle.
- Seat and lower body seem heavier and secure.
- Tensions that block the flow of energy through your body are released.
- You will be relaxed and ready for the next movement or exercise.

## Building Blocks

The last of the Four Basics I call building blocks, which is a way of describing balance. If you balance the various parts of the body correctly, one above the other, you will reduce the amount of muscle tension or strain used to keep the body upright and, in doing so, save the energy for other uses. You will find that building blocks tie in so closely with the other Basics—soft eyes, breathing, and centering—they are difficult to learn and master unless all four are practiced together.

I like to think of the building blocks as children's wooden blocks. You can make them different colors in your mind, if you like. The point is that building blocks must balance one above the other. (Fig. 14.) If they are not carefully balanced, they become unstable, or worse yet, fall down in a heap. (Fig. 15.)

Your bottom building block is your legs and feet. The next block is your pelvis, then rib cage, shoulders, and last, your head and neck. For flat work, the correct lineup of the blocks (viewing the body sideways) will allow you to drop a plumb line from the ear through the tip of the shoulder, hip joint, and ankle. (Fig. 16.) Just before it passes through your hip joint, you will find it going straight through your center.

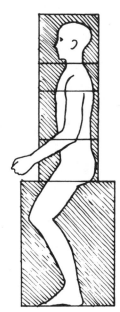

14. *Building blocks must be carefully balanced, one above the other.*

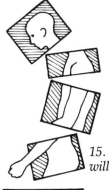

15. *If blocks are not balanced, they will fall down.*

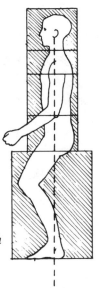

16. *Plumb line dropping through building blocks.*

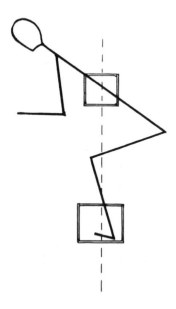

When standing on the ground your center must be over your feet or you will fall down. That is also true in any correct riding position. But you don't always need all the blocks. For example, in a jumping or galloping seat, instead of five blocks you only need to line up two—your center and your feet. (Figs. 17a & b.) The mass of your hips stays behind the plumb line to offset the weight of your forward-reaching head and shoulders.

To be able to balance your building blocks correctly, there are two important variables that need to be adjusted properly. The first is the length of your stirrups. It varies according to the conformation of the rider and the horse, and also with the type of saddle used. If you are using an all-purpose or forward-seat saddle, you must ride shorter than you would on a dressage saddle. But if you do have a dressage saddle, don't be carried away by the feeling that you must ride with very long stirrups. Balance and efficiency in the use of the legs is the key. When your legs are in the correct position, your feet should rest lightly but flat in the stirrups. If you find you must reach for your stirrups, they are too long; your feet will swing forward and you will lose your bottom building block. If you are long-legged and/or your horse is round and shallow-bodied, you will need to shorten the stirrups in order to reach his sides with your legs. Your stirrup leathers will probably be at least two or three holes longer for flat work than for galloping or jumping, but must still hang straight, behind your knee and in front of your ankle, with your hip joint over your ankle. If you have heavy thighs, you'll have to ride with shorter stirrups. Accept the fact or lose weight, but don't compromise your riding.

*17a & b. Even in the galloping seat, the center must be over the feet.*

The second variable is the saddle. Many saddles are designed so that balance is impossible, given the conformation of your horse. For proper building blocks, a correctly balanced saddle is needed. (Figs. 18a–e.) This is why you see so many saddles boosted up behind with foam rubber pads or cushions. The lowest part of the saddle must be in the middle, close to the pommel. If it is too far back, there is no way you can ride in good building-block form, so don't hesitate to join the legions using foam rubber under the cantle or a well-made wedge-

18. *The same saddle on different horses.*

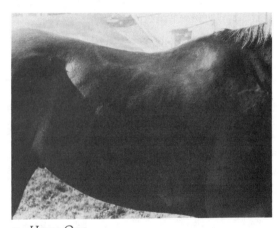

*a. Horse One.*

*b. The saddle fits.*

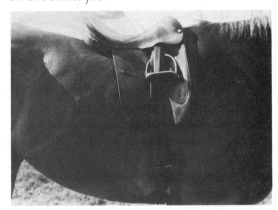

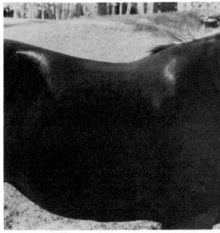

*c. Horse Two.*

*d. The saddle sits too low in back because he is wider in the withers.*

*e. Balance of the saddle corrected on Horse Two by inserting foam rubber cushion under the back of the saddle. Though it now looks too high in the back, the foam rubber will squash down sufficiently with the rider's weight.*

shaped pad. Be sure to insert the cushion between the saddle pad and the saddle. Do not use a blanket or towels under the cantle or your horse will develop a tender back. Best of all, though not always possible, get a saddle that will properly fit your horse.

## What are the essentials of building blocks?
- Balanced body, from feet through head.
- Properly adjusted stirrup leathers.
- Correctly balanced saddle.

## What are the results of building blocks?
- Consistent balance with the horse's movement.
- Fluid and comfortable motion of the horse.

Now you have the Four Basics: soft eyes, breathing, centering, and building blocks. So try trotting your horse, rising to the trot, allowing all your weight to go through to your stirrups. Don't block your downward weight by pinching with your knees or any part of your legs. Let your legs rest softly against the horse's sides. Use your hip and knee joints freely so you can feel the full up and down motion of the rising trot.

Using soft eyes, breathing, and centering, check yourself to see if your building blocks are truly correct. If your center is behind, your head and feet will probably be forward and your horse will be trying to catch up with both of them. If only your feet are forward, you will be coming down too heavily on the cantle of your saddle and your horse will not like that.

Try this exercise: Post one beat, stay up on the stirrups for two beats, post one, stay up two. Do this continuously. If you are not balanced over your stirrups, you will bang down on your horse and will be forced to stay down more than one beat. But when you really find the correct balance and rhythm, this exercise is like a dance.

Allow your body to come into balance as you trot. Give it time. Let your center of gravity drop, and think about your breathing and your center of energy. On each rise try to feel that you have a spring pulling your center (or your

*19. Feel a spring pulling your cen-ter forward to the sky.*

belt buckle) diagonally upward and forward toward the sky. (Fig. 19.) Gradually your center will come forward and, as it does, your legs and feet will move back under you. Your body will become more erect, with your shoulders and head no longer leading. You will now be able to come down in your trot more lightly and farther forward on the saddle. This balance is easier on your horse. He would prefer to carry you over the stirrup bars rather than feel you bouncing backward, down on the cantle.

The usual comments by my students at this point are: "It is so much easier." "I feel so much lighter." "It is no effort." "I feel so *with* my horse."

The horse usually has something to say, too. The rapid, high-headed horse who has been trying to catch up to his rider's head and shoulders in order to avoid the bumps on his back will gradually relax; his strides will become slower and longer; his head will go down and his back come up. The lethargic horse, on the other hand, will begin to move forward more freely, with longer strides, and become more alert. You and your horse feel more fluid as you come into balance with each other. Both of you start to become the lovely ideal of the horse-person, not just a person on a horse.

# 4

# Learning and the Brain

The ability to use the Four Basics successfully depends upon the functions of the brain and learning. The brain is divided lengthwise into two separate halves, the right and the left. They are connected by the corpus callosum, a two-way bridge of nerve fibers between the halves. The right- and left-brain concept, as outlined below, will help our awareness and learning patterns.

In general, each side of the brain has its own functions. The left side is the practical side. It likes to handle things in a linear manner, organizing and arranging the details of life. It likes to be rational, analytical, and verbal. It is the busy side of the brain in the technical world that surrounds us. The right brain deals with much larger areas, in wholes instead of parts. It is intuitive and full of imagery. It likes to integrate and synthesize, allowing things to happen simultaneously, and has little use for words.

Have you had times of physical activity when your body gave you pure joy, when what you did seemed infinitely easy and correct? Maybe it was that perfect fluid tennis stroke, or perhaps a flawless run down a ski trail. These are the breakthrough moments when the right brain is allowed to take over the responsiveness of your body with no interference from the left brain.

If we use a left-brain approach to riding a circle, for instance, and list all the six or seven details needed, we'd be halfway around the circle before we finished the list. Because of the way our language works, we are forced to think and talk about the aids in a linear sequence and fragment the information or activity into sections.

When the right brain, however, controls the activity, the muscles of the body respond automatically, with simultaneous and synchronized movements to whole-image directions.

Unfortunately, all too often the left brain will interfere. Its chatter interrupts, "You never get your outside leg on steadily enough" or "My horse'll veer toward the barn as always, and lose his rhythm by the gate." Often the left brain will bring in something totally inappropriate, like "I forgot to brush my teeth this morning!" Horrors! Concentration and synthesis of the aids are lost.

Actually, the brain halves do not have to be in constant battle. If correctly used, they become equal halves moving and molding against each other, like oil and water in a glass ball will change shape and mold and flow around each other, yet stay the same in quantity. (Fig. 20.) They become unopposing opposites, different but working as one. The only trouble is that you often overuse the left brain at the expense of the right. So now you must consciously learn to use the right brain in a trusting, relaxed way. You must learn to fight less and flow more.

20. *Oil and water, in a moving glass ball, continually flow and reshape but never blend.*

To make a circle, for instance, each of the many necessary aids must first be learned separately by the left brain. Start by letting the left brain analyze the position of the pelvis and seat bones and discover how this feels and looks. Then, with soft eyes, let the sensations settle in your right brain. Add to these the placement and timing of the legs, then the use of your shoulders, arms, and hands, and the position of your head. Each image you build into the right brain must include not only how you and your horse will look, but how your body will feel under you, and even how the horse's feet will sound. Feel, sight, sound, and rhythm are all one complete package. Each new or corrected detail dropped into the right brain will become a part of a synchronized function—no longer a one-two-three process.

It is important to realize from the beginning that imagery can influence muscles. Muscles can be brought into action or released by images without discernible motion. In this way the quality of control of the arm, leg, or whatever, can be improved and eventually, through practice, become automatic. To achieve this goal, it is first necessary to isolate each part of the body so the rider may learn how that part functions and how it feels when it moves correctly and incorrectly. This bit-by-bit approach gives the rider an understanding of the role each body part plays. Then an increasingly efficient use of the body becomes possible. This learning process actually develops quite rapidly, assuming each section is understood before going to the next. To let the right brain take over, trust is essential—trust in your body, your horse, and the ability of your right brain to assimilate all the correct information.

## Inner Video

An inner videotape can help. This is a private videotape inside you. To play it, use your soft eyes and, in your mind, see, hear, and feel an entire movement or exercise before actually doing it. It can also be useful to play your videotape continuously during a movement and then replay it afterward to check any errors. Try this: Before doing a circle, as you center yourself and organize your breathing, play your videotape of the whole movement of your horse-person and then trust and allow your body to function without tension and fear; the hard-eyed left brain will gradually become quieter and stop interfering. This does not mean you don't use your aids actively. You do, but the parts of your body will cooperate and will move with less effort.

How did your circle feel? Was it smooth and open? How did it sound? Were the horse's feet light or heavy on the ground? How did it look? Was it round, or was it oval, pear-shaped, a spiral, or perhaps even had a corner? Did that devilish left brain interfere? On your internal video-tape, replay the circle as you rode it. There are probably some unclear spots. These are the parts that were not quite right. So take those spots out of the tape and throw them away. They are past, and you don't want to worry about them again. If you worry about them, they will get in the way.

Having thrown away the incorrect parts, edit a new section into your tape and, playing it correctly, ride another circle. The minute you've ridden it, use your instant replay again to see how that one went. If there are still some unclear sections, repeat the editing process, set in the good images, and replay. Each time you do this, you are deleting from your right brain the wrong "footage" and replacing it with what is correct. As you progress to more precise work, your videotape images will become more complex, but no harder to carry out if you have trained your body and right brain through constant repetition and correction. Your body eventually develops the ability to respond to any image your videotape plays. Remember that as you begin learning a new technique, the images should be simple, and the right and left brain, soft and hard eyes, centering, and breathing just all work together.

You can learn your video routines without being on a horse. Let's say you have had one of those frustrating riding days where everything seemed to go wrong. It would be extremely useful, later on, in peace and quiet, to play all the riding sequences over and over as you knew they *should* have been. Next time you ride, the problems actually vanish—movement occurs easily, rhythmically, and correctly. By playing your edited videotape, you have clarified the new movement in the right brain. This is a known psychological phenomenon called covert learning.

## Concentration

In order to learn most efficiently, you must be able to concentrate. You can't force yourself to concentrate, however; if you do, you will immediately find yourself tense—with a scowling face, set jaw, and tight shoulders, holding your breath, with your center of gravity rising. This is hard work. This is the left brain being busy and getting in the way. Most people want to be in total mental control of everything they do and find it difficult to allow their bodies to function without step-by-step instruction from the left brain.

Watch a child or puppy playing. It has total concentration on whatever it's doing, be it chewing on a toy, chasing a ball, or building with blocks and throwing them down again. (Fig. 21.) The concentration may shift from

21. *A child lost in total concentration, playing with his toy blocks.*

one thing to another, but when it's there, it is total, complete, relaxed, and happy. In total concentration like this, the left brain is not interfering. Children and animals have not overdeveloped the left brain as you most likely have. Your goal is to allow yourself to concentrate just like puppies and small children.

Betty Edwards, in her book *Drawing on the Right Side of the Brain,* tells us how she found that drawing seems to be a right-brained activity. She describes her state of concentration: "I have always done a lot of demonstration drawing in my classes, and it was my wish during the demonstrations to explain to students what I was doing—what I was looking at, why I was drawing things in certain ways. I often found, however, that I would simply stop talking right in the middle of a sentence. I would hear my voice stop and I would think about getting back to the sentence, but finding the words again would seem like a terrible chore—and I didn't really want to anyhow. But, pulling myself back at last, I would resume talking—and then find I had lost contact with the drawing, which suddenly seemed confusing and difficult. Thus I picked up a new bit of information: I could either talk or draw, but I couldn't do both at once."

I have had riders who were able to work in this state of true concentration. I can suggest things to them that they will incorporate instantly into their physical work, but they do not or cannot respond verbally until later. Their descriptions of how they felt during that time tend to be vague, though I can see in their eyes that they are still feeling those satisfying sensations.

How do you achieve this happy state of concentration? For some the path is more difficult than for others. Outside elements batter at the door all the time: the stirrups feel wrong, a dog starts barking, your horse sees a gremlin behind a tree, a gust of wind comes along. The way to deal with these left-brain intrusions is to accept them as facts and immediately disregard them without further consideration. Do not argue. The stirrups really are okay, the dog does no harm, the gremlin disappears, and the wind makes no difference. (Fig. 22.) Your riding awareness and concentration have hardly been disrupted after all.

22. *When you concentrate,*
*distractions are of no concern.*

You can practice in a playful way. Let's ride a circle again. Using your videotape, switch back and forth between the left and right brain, center yourself (right brain) with breathing and soft eyes, then place your legs correctly (left brain). Now center yourself again, recheck the placing of your legs, and so on, back and forth. It should be easy and fun, like a game, not dull and frustrating. Soon you will find that you play less with the legs because their placing has become coordinated and simultaneous with the centering. There you are, joyfully concentrating on doing circles. You have opened yourself and let the concentration happen. It probably would not have happened if you had rigidly decided, "Now I'm going to concentrate on circles."

## Awareness and Self-Exploration

The object of my teaching is to enable the pupil to absorb the offered information and then use it independently. All too often a student becomes dependent on my presence. Before you can work effectively alone, you must have a sound knowledge of how your body performs. Once you have this grounding, I can help you achieve increased awareness and greater independence.

Until about the age of two, bodies move in a natural way. From then on the customs of society tend to inhibit natural movement. For example, a child sitting in an ill-fitting chair is told to stop wiggling, though a healthy body wants and needs to wiggle when in discomfort. Social situations create a multitude of incorrect muscular patterns that most of us live with all our lives. The next exploration-exercise helps to dispel the bad habits and allow the normal, correct ones to take over.

You probably often concentrate too much on a single problem spot, feeling that it must be corrected before you can move on. But as you struggle to make that correction, you neglect the rest of the body, which becomes distorted, full of tension, and out of balance. When you begin to feel this kind of discomfort, try exploring your whole body, section by section. Don't dwell on any one part. You may make some surprising discoveries, or none at all. Don't worry, just accept whatever comes. People with short, squat bodies who would like to be tall and slim may find their bodies asking for more room. An ineffective left leg may tell you that the tension in your right hip, or even in your neck, is the real trouble. A problem you've never been aware of may become evident.

Whenever you put your awareness on a particular part of the body, you drop some energy into that part. You should not waste that energy by trying to make a specific forced correction on that original problem spot, because this will make you dwell on an incorrect habit. The right technique is to move your awareness quickly to some other body area. The energy left behind can then be used to correct the problem. It will allow you to use muscles you previously did not know how to use.

To watch a student work through this exploration is fascinating. You can see the rider's body becoming softer, more fluid, taller, more balanced, legs longer and more supple, ankles and knees soft, hands sensitive. The exercise demonstrates that if you remove the muscular and nervous interferences you build into your body, you will begin to function naturally, in a more balanced and efficient manner.

When one girl told me that she could do what I taught her about 90 percent of the time when with me, but only about 40 percent when alone, I realized I must give my students some better tools to take away with them. She practiced the above exercise in self-awareness diligently for the duration of the lesson. By the end she was deliriously happy. She had never ridden so well, and her horse had never been so forward-moving, light, and balanced. Most important, however, was her feeling that she could use this technique anywhere, anytime—take her instruction with her and be independent.

### What are the essentials of learning and concentration?

- Use your hard eyes and left brain to identify the correct functions and feelings of a particular movement.
- Use your soft eyes and right brain to allow that feeling to become integrated in the right brain as a part of the whole.
- Don't dwell long on any one problem area in your own or your horse's body.

### What are the results?

- The parts of a movement will be synchronized into a whole.
- Your body will respond with less effort and will function correctly.

# 5

## Anatomy

**W**hy must you understand your skeletal structure in order to ride a horse? Not many riders think much about their bones, except perhaps for their seat bones. Everyone seems to concentrate on muscles. Actually, the balance of one grouping of bones above another, all up and down the body, as well as the articulation of the joints of the skeleton, must be correct to produce a balanced and coordinated rider. If the bones are in the right place, then the muscles need to do less work, resulting in fewer tensions. A frequent comment that I love to hear from my students is, "I am learning to ride with my bones. It is much easier that way to stay supple." (Fig. 23.) Knowledge about the lungs, diaphragm, and other major muscles can increase awareness—and therefore control—of the body movements.

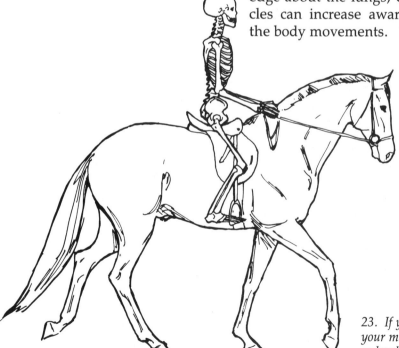

23. *If you "ride with your bones," your muscles won't have to work so hard.*

## *The Pelvis and Below*

The pelvis is the foundation of the riding seat. It is a collection of bones pretty much fused together in a shape rather like a bowl with no bottom. The lower spine is fused into the back of the pelvis at the sacrum—that big hard bone you can easily feel with your fingers. This means that weight from above will be transmitted through the spine and sacrum down the back of the pelvis. The legs, on the other hand, connect in the mobile hip joints that are located more forward in the pelvis. The seat bones are directly below the hip joints, so whether standing or sitting, the thrust from below goes up the front of the pelvis.

Behind the seat bones and below the coccyx (the last bit of the spine below the sacrum) lie the buttocks. When the pelvis is correctly leveled you will sit on both your seat bones and your buttocks. The pelvis forms a bridge or cantilever between your spine and your seat bones, allowing a slight cushioning spring between the two. (Fig. 24.)

The legs come up to the middle of the pelvis on both sides. The head of the femur is round like a ball, and this ball fits into a deep, very smooth, round socket above the seat bones in the pelvis. (Fig. 25.) This juncture between

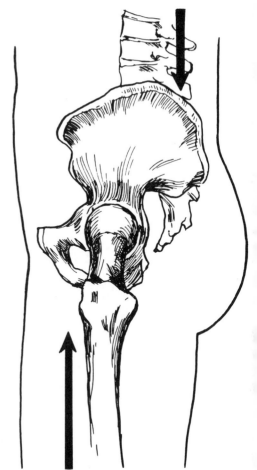

24. *The pelvis as seen from the side, showing the weight of the spine going down the back and the thrust from the legs going up the front.*

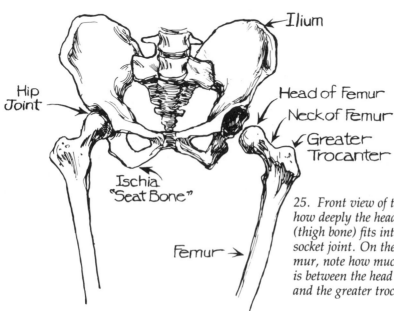

25. *Front view of the pelvis. Note how deeply the head of the femur (thigh bone) fits into its ball-and-socket joint. On the detached femur, note how much length there is between the head of the femur and the greater trochanter.*

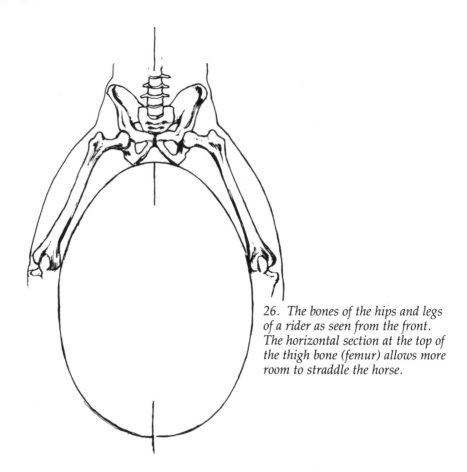

*26. The bones of the hips and legs of a rider as seen from the front. The horizontal section at the top of the thigh bone (femur) allows more room to straddle the horse.*

*27. The hip joint has great freedom of movement.*

the leg and the pelvis—called a ball-and-socket joint—is all covered with cartilage. Cartilage against cartilage is as slippery as ice on ice. From the hip joint in the pelvis, the thigh bone (femur) travels two to three inches out to the side to a point called the greater trochanter before it drops down to the knee. Conveniently, these extra inches give you more openness of leg to straddle your horse's back. (Fig. 26.) Because of this positioning, the formation is very free moving and gives the leg a tremendous radius of motion, but only if we allow it to. (Fig. 27.) A professional ballet or modern dancer can make a full circle with the leg coming near the shoulder in the arc. Olympic figure skaters can hold one foot directly over their heads. Most people, however, do not use the joint nearly to its capacity, but instead inhibit the motion with tight muscles so that it becomes inelastic. The hip joint is of great importance since all downward pressure from above as well as all upthrusts from below must go through it.

Try to find exactly where the hip joint is with your hand. (Fig. 28.) Lift your knee up and down while you search for the bend of the joint with your fingers. The joint is probably much lower than you thought. You will feel a cord that lines up with the top of your knee tighten under your fingers. The joint is just under the inner side of that cord. Continue wiggling the leg around until you are sure you know and can feel where the joint is—low and definitely in front.

Put the palm of your hand over the side seam of your pants and rotate your leg: You should be able to feel the greater trochanter moving. (Fig. 29.) Imagine a flipper rotating in the hip joint (Fig. 30), or a gate hanging down from only the upper hinge. The gate hangs heavily from one hinge, but you can still close the gate. (Fig. 31.) The relationship of the femur to the hip joint and pelvis, and potential movement within this area, can be understood through these images. You can rotate the thigh using a lot of muscle and tension; or you can use soft eyes, play your internal videotape, and see the greater trochanter move forward *through* the muscles—as if a string were gently pulling it, rotating the femur from the very top. This can be done with very little muscular involvement. You must use soft eyes and see it inwardly.

28. *Finding the hip joint. Left hand points to the hip joint; right hand points to the ilium, or hip bone.*

29. *Finding the greater trochanter under the palm of the hand.*

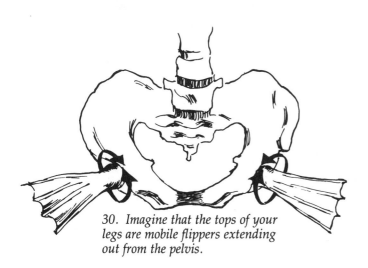

30. *Imagine that the tops of your legs are mobile flippers extending out from the pelvis.*

31. *Imagine that your leg is like a gate hanging down from only the upper hinge (your hip joint).*

*32a. Pelvis rolled forward, causing a hollow lower back and rounded shoulders.*

*b. Pelvis correctly balanced, resulting in the normal slight curves of the spine and a straight, strong back.*

*c. Pelvis rolled backward, causing a rounded back and shoulders, a collapsed chest, and protruding head.*

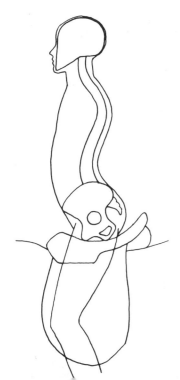
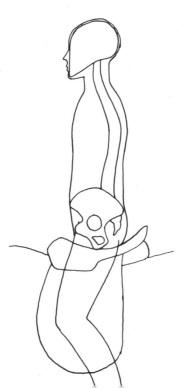
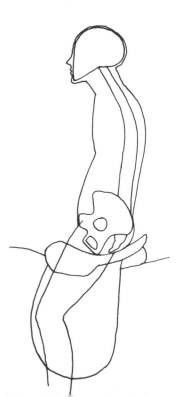

Whether sitting or standing, movement of the pelvis is intimately related to movement of the lower back and hip joints. When you hollow your lower back, you are going to tip the front of your pelvis down and the back up, because the spine is fused to the back of the pelvis. (Figs. 32a–c.) This movement will alter the angle between the leg and the pelvis at the hip joint. It will also place the sacrum over the seat bones so that any cushioning is lost. If you round your lower back, however, the tilt will reverse. Thus, anything you do with the lower back affects the pelvis and hip joints; conversely, anything you do with the pelvis affects the lower back and hip joints. But your legs can affect the hip joints without affecting anything else.

Sitting on your horse, without stirrups, place your hand against your lower back, the five vertebrae of the lumbar spine, between your ribs and pelvis. (Fig. 33.) This part of the back should be straight or have a very small curve forward. If yours is hollow (curved forward), move your entire pelvis forward in the saddle, which brings your seat bones forward. Relax your lower back, allowing it to lengthen. This will bring your buttocks onto the saddle, which will fill the space vacated when you moved forward. Most people find, to their surprise, that they are more comfortable and relaxed in this new position.

It's important to remember that a soft, straight lower back is your objective. If you hollow the lower back, you will feel tension in that area immediately. You don't want tension, so relax it again. Put your awareness in your hip joints and upper thighs, and hollow your back again. Notice how tension enters the hip joints, tending to lift the thighs upward.

If you round your lower back (the opposite of hollowing), you will need to think a great deal about feeling your center and lumbar spine moving forward and up. This will help to straighten your spine and tip your pelvis forward, lowering it in front so it will be level and you will no longer be on the back of your buttocks.

33. *Fingers on the lumbar spine.*

Think about the comfort of your horse. Would he prefer two hard seat bones on his back carrying all your weight? Or would he rather feel the weight spread more evenly around on the greater bearing surface of your softer seat bones as well as your buttocks? I am sure you will agree that he prefers the latter.

Next, try this exercise: Walk your horse without stirrups. Sit on your seat bones and your buttocks as described above, and feel the thrust of movement in your horse's back. Feel what happens when you *let the horse move you*. Completely relax your buttocks and backs of your thighs. All the muscles of your back between your belt and the saddle must be soft and supple; your stomach muscles also. Do not create the motion. Just allow the horse to move you. Check your lower back with your hand to feel if it is soft and quiet, and then the hip joint to see if it is moving freely.

## Knees and Lower Legs

While sitting on your horse, pretend that instead of having a lower leg and foot you have a weight on the end of a string, hung from the bottom of your thigh. (Fig. 34.) Try to swing this weight forward and back without touching the horse. In the same way, let both your lower legs swing forward and back from the knees, feet relaxed, as if each were like the weight on the string. Don't *pull* your legs back and *push* them forward. Just give them a start and try to let them keep going under their own momentum. Then swing them alternate ways on the two sides. When you have a nice free feeling, swing them the same way on both sides—both legs forward, both legs back.

Now, for contrast, instead of swinging your legs, push them forward and pull them back with knee muscles, pausing between each back-and-forth motion. You will find it requires much more effort and feels very stiff and tense when compared to the free swing. This freedom of the knee is what you will need later in sitting to the trot and canter. It is a feeling you must become familiar with.

*34. Keep your knee free, as if your whole lower leg was only a weight hanging from the end of a string.*

Next, relax the legs and make big circles with your ankles and feet so that the bottoms of your feet look in all directions—forward, out, back, in—both clockwise and counterclockwise. (Fig. 35.) Don't let the muscles beside your shin (bone in the front of the leg, between knee and ankle) get tight. Your lower legs must hang limp from your knees. You should have a lot of motion in your ankles and feet. Get your toes into it, too, by spreading them sideways in your boots. Even cock your little toe out and up as your foot spirals around. Imitate the prim ladies who drink tea with their pinkies delicately cocked—only do it now with your toes. The toes will love it. Feel that your feet are active, your ankles supple and soft.

Now you can add some whole-leg exercises to help coordinate your pelvis and legs. Alternately allow one leg to swing back and the other forward from the hip like a pair of scissors. Each time the leg goes back, sink your heel toward the horse's hind foot. This exercise opens the hip joint. Small motions are sufficient; it is important not to hollow or tense your back or tighten your buttocks, since this will result in twisting the pelvis, which lifts the seat bone, buttock, and the back of the leg as you stretch.

*35. Keep your leg and knee relaxed while rotating your foot.*

Do the swings three times back and forth while you search for the feeling that you are balancing with the seat bones and the buttocks softly on the saddle while not involving the upper body.

The next exercise is to try swinging one leg straight out sideways from the horse and dropping it. Don't hold the leg away—just throw it out and drop it. Viewed sideways, it should go out directly under your pelvis and ear. After you get the feeling with one leg, you can try both legs at once. (Fig. 36.) You don't have to reach out very far. The looser you are, the easier it is. For some people this is a very difficult exercise. If you find it so, don't do too much at one time. Avoid strain!

Again, with your legs in a comfortable position, and sitting centered on your saddle, try lifting one heel and lower leg up toward your buttock as if you were going to kick yourself in the seat; then drop it again. Did you feel the buttock and thigh tighten? Try it again, but this time imagine lifting your foot by a string tied to your heel. (Fig. 37.) You really have to concentrate on this, using soft eyes, breathing, and centering. Try not to use your buttock and

*36. Swinging both legs out sideways.*

*37. Lift your lower leg toward your buttock.*

thigh muscles. Let the string do the work. Move your leg up a little and drop it again before the muscles tighten. Do this several times. With each lift you should be able to raise the heel higher, and keep it there longer, without tension. When you can do it well with one leg, practice with the other, and then with both at once with your arms stretched out sideways. Notice that as you do this better you will find your buttocks coming more underneath you and your thighs and knees wanting to hang down without pinching against the saddle, giving you a feeling of a very deep seat.

By now you should feel comfortable from the waist down, with no more tight muscles and tensions. You should feel *wide* and *settled* through the seat bones, buttocks, and backs of your thighs. Your lower back should feel long and soft. Your legs should be comfortable around the horse. There should be motion in all parts of the lower body in rhythm with the horse—a nice balanced feeling.

## The Pelvis and Above

The spine rises upward from the back of the pelvis. It has several forward and backward curves. If you look carefully at the side profile of the spine, you will notice that the curves of the front of the spine are more pronounced than those of the back, especially in the lumbar area, where the vertebrae become thicker. (Fig. 38.) In addition, because of the heavy muscles of the lumbar area, the lower back, as seen from the side of a correctly balanced body, will be straight or nearly so. The spine through the thorax (rib cage) may have a slight backward curve but should not have a forward hollow. The seven smaller cervical vertebrae in the neck have a graceful forward curve leading up to the head.

It is very important that the spinal curves balance each other and be neither too extreme nor too straight. If you thrust your head forward, you will automatically push out the spine beneath your shoulder blades in order to balance your head. You will then counterbalance that bulge by

*38. The curves of the spine are more pronounced in front than in back, owing to the different thicknesses of parts of the spine.*

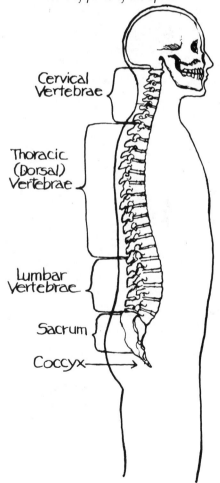

Cervical Vertebrae

Thoracic (Dorsal) Vertebrae

Lumbar Vertebrae

Sacrum

Coccyx

41

hollowing your lower back. As a result, your pubic arch, the front of your pelvis, will drop down and your buttocks will tilt up behind. What I am describing anatomically is the ordinary slouch position. The initial problem that creates the slouch is usually protrusion of the head. To balance the head correctly, you can't simply pull it back. You must reduce the curves of both your thorax and lumbar (lower) spine, bringing the whole alignment back to normal. Once the spine is allowed to be long and the curves are correct, the pelvis will hang naturally in a level position.

*39. Pull straight up on some hair directly on top of your head above your ears.*

To achieve this spinal length, imagine you are hanging on a string from the top of your head like a puppet. With your hand, pull straight up on some hair directly on top of your head between your ears. As you pull you will feel your face hanging perpendicular; the front of your neck will feel soft and the back of your neck will be slightly stretched. If you pull hair that is too far forward, your chin will protrude and the front of your neck will feel full. If you pull hair that is too far back, the front of your neck will be squashed by your chin. Pull the hair correctly until you are sure of the balanced feel. (Fig. 39.) At that point, use your imagination to create the upward pull, and simultaneously release the spine to its full length. Be aware of the correct feeling and allow the natural movement to come through.

Not all parts of the spine have equal mobility. The neck has the most freedom to move. The thoracic vertebrae have some motion, but are restricted by the encumbrance of the ribs. The lumbar spine has considerable freedom forward, backward, and sideways.

Shoulders are composed of a complex of bones called the shoulder girdle, because they go all *around* the top of the ribs. The two collarbones create the front of the girdle and the shoulder blades create the rear. The shoulder girdle is attached to the ribs at only one point, where ligaments connect the collarbones to the top of the sternum (breastbone) like a hinge. Thus the shoulders are free-moving, hanging from muscles attached to the head and neck.

Keeping this last image in mind, try the following exercise: Make big, free, easy circles with your shoulders; move them slowly up toward your ears and then the back; let them drop totally free. As you do this exercise, feel how much the shoulder blades move around over the ribs and almost touch each other as you go through the up-back-drop part of the circle. (Figs. 40a–c.) It should be an open, relaxing exercise without any tension in the shoulder girdle. Be sure to balance your head as you make the circles.

You will find that this exercise can be used as a quick and simple means to reestablish, without effort, the correct relaxed posture for your shoulders, arms, and head. If you drop the shoulders loosely, they will fall below your ears where they belong; your arms will hang from them, free for activity. People who carry their shoulders too far forward—a common habit—are frequently told to draw their shoulders back and throw out the chest, forcing the blades together. This position creates rigidity, and thus tension, all down the back of the body. What you want instead is a supple, free body that can move and balance with your horse. If you inhibit pulling the shoulders forward, you will allow their natural open position to take over.

During a dressage test, I watched one of my students become tense due to shoulders pulled forward. The horse moved with diminishing motion. At a corner the rider freed herself (and the horse) with a quick up-back-drop of the shoulders. She went on to complete a fine test that had been on its way to mediocrity.

40. *Shoulder girdle and rib cage as seen from above.*

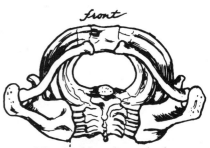

a. *The shoulders drawn back, bringing the shoulder blades close together. This position creates tension.*

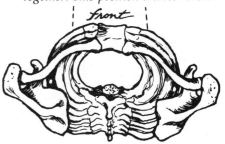

b. *The shoulders hanging correctly.*

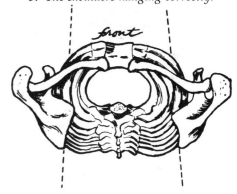

c. *The shoulders drawn forward, with the shoulder blades pulled apart. In this position the back tends to bulge between them and the sternum is pushed down by the collarbones, depressing the chest.*

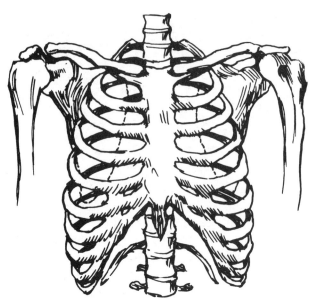

41a & b. *The shoulder girdle is like a yoke across the top of the ribs. The arms are the ropes carrying the pails.*

Think of your shoulders again. This time imagine a yoke as it might lie across your shoulders. (Figs. 41a & b.) It sticks out beyond them and from underneath hang ropes that are tied to buckets of water or milk. Your shoulders and arms are much like this yoke. The collarbones and shoulder blades meet at the tips of the shoulders, sticking out beyond the ribs, and the arms hang from underneath. Imagine one arm being the rope of the yoke and swing it freely. To do this, you will have to relax and release the muscles all around the tip of your shoulder. Keep swinging that arm—or both arms if that is easier for you—until you feel a smooth, rhythmic motion, with no restrictions from the shoulder muscles.

If you have difficulty doing this, hang one arm loosely, tighten the muscles hard around the end of your shoulder, and make a clenched fist. Slowly count to five, then relax the shoulder and hand completely. After repeating this three times, you will feel the bones of the arm to be more separate and free from the bones of the shoulder girdle. You should then really be able to swing the arm like a bucket hanging from a yoke.

When the shoulders hang balanced and open, notice that the ends of the shoulder blades settle down flat against the ribs. (Fig. 42.) On the other hand, if you round your back, bringing the tips of the shoulders forward, the shoulder blades will stick out somewhat like wings, a sight we see very often. In doing this, the collarbones are brought together and, for lack of room, push the ends that are hinged on the sternum, taking down with them the sternum and front of the ribs, which ultimately puts pressure on the lungs, diaphragm, stomach, liver, and so on. What a mess! This is all part of that old familiar slouch position.

To rectify this, visualize your collarbones. Allow them to flow out sideways, horizontally. Don't push them, just let them grow and drift out there, way beyond your body, right out into the fields and trees. This will gently allow the sternum and ribs to come up, the front of the body to relax, the shoulders to hang easily, and the whole body to become more open, balanced, and free. Allowing the collarbones to widen and the lower back to lengthen are two wonderful sensations. Adding them to the feeling of the total body moving in unison with the horse is even more satisfying.

## Ribs

Under the umbrella of the shoulder girdle lie the ribs. Each pair of ribs, right and left, hangs from a spinal vertebra. From there, they curve out around toward the front of the body. The ribs are attached to the sternum in front by movable cartilage. The upper ribs come around almost horizontally, and the lower ribs slope increasingly downward as they come forward with longer and longer cartilage between the ends of the ribs and the sternum. The last two pairs of ribs, the floating ribs, aren't attached to anything and come around only to the middle of your sides. You can feel where they end if you poke around your side at the bottom of the rib cage. Find also the bottom of your sternum with your fingers. It is at the front of your diaphragm.

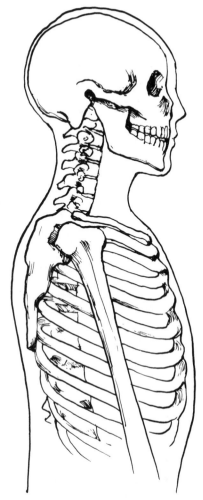

42. *Shoulder blades lying flat against the ribs.*

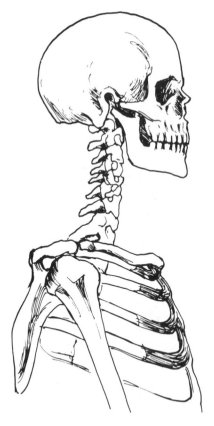

The attachment of the ribs to the vertebrae allows some limited motion in the back, both up and down and backward and forward. At the front of the ribs, however, the motion is considerably greater, owing to the long cartilage. I like to think of each rib as a door. The hinge side of the door, which is the part attached to the spine, does not move very much, but the latch side of the door, the front of the rib, moves a lot. The front and sides of our ribs are able to move much more than many of us realize. Each time you breathe in with your diaphragm, the inhaled air will softly lift and spread the rib cage and drop it again as you exhale. If you can keep this feeling of elasticity and freedom all through your upper body, your riding will improve immeasurably.

## The Neck and Head

The neck comes up through the shoulder girdle, and the head balances on top. The bones that you can feel at the back of your neck are called spinous processes, and do not carry weight. The weight-bearing part is the inner section of the vertebrae, called the body. This part connects with your head between the lobes of your ears. (Fig. 43.) The ears are central, and there is a lot of head behind them. To better comprehend this new idea, make the tiniest wobbly motions with your head (not using your neck) sideways, forward, and back until you begin to sense the central connection of the head and neck. Your jaw swings from just under the ears. Make sure that your jaw is not clenched, but is free, and that your eyes are up and relaxed, looking straight ahead. If you feel that the top of your sternum is light and high, it will be easier to keep your neck and head balanced.

43. *The head balances on the neck at a point just between your ears.*

44. *Balance your head like a billiard ball on the end of a cue stick.*

As you make these tiny motions, pretend your head is a billiard ball and you are balancing it on the end of a pool cue. (Fig. 44.) When you are riding, there is motion all the time, and you therefore have to keep rebalancing the ball on the stick. You could glue the billiard ball onto the stick and it would stay put, no harm done. But your head glued to your neck would create all kinds of tensions, and tensions are what you are trying to eliminate. So let's not use glue, let's use balance!

If you balance your head correctly, you will discover that you can feel its weight going through your spine right to the seat bones and buttocks, which ultimately provide the base from which the head is balanced. Give yourself time to find and recognize that sensation. You will feel that your face is perpendicular and that the center of your head is sitting comfortably on the top of your neck.

Now that you have your head and shoulders nicely balanced, let's use the head as a tool. It weighs approximately ten to fifteen pounds. And if you think about carrying fifteen pounds of oats held out and away from your side, you know that it is an appreciable weight. Try this exercise: As you walk on your horse, drop your head straight down and let it hang—dead weight. (Fig. 45.) Use it to stretch the back of the spine. You can do this with the help of your soft eyes and inner video. You may or may not wish to bend the back, depending upon which position allows you to relax the most. Feel the back of your spine stretching, vertebra by vertebra, through the neck area, then down between the shoulder blades, making sure the latter area gets loosened up. Then let your stretch extend to the diaphragm and lower ribs. This can be a difficult spot, so stay there mentally long enough to really feel things letting go. Keep breathing as you do this. Finally, try to stretch the spine below the ribs in the lumbar area, and keep going right on down to the coccyx (the tailbone at the base of your spine). Give yourself ample time to do this exercise, thinking of your body and spine, part by part, until you get to the bottom.

Now sit up, balance, and drop your head back. (Fig. 46.) Stretch the front of the spine and the body, starting at the neck. Where the collarbones meet, imagine you can spread them apart as well as stretch the area up and down. Continue the image of stretching and opening the front of the ribs. When you reach the diaphragm at the bottom of the ribs, allow it to expand forward and sideways. Relax your stomach, so it becomes longer. You will have stretched the body from chin to pubic arch. Sit up again.

Do each of the above exercises a second time and you will find you can go much more rapidly down the spine to

45. *Let your head drop straight forward and hang like a dead weight to help stretch the spine.*

46. *Drop your head back to open the front of the body.*

get the same sensations. You can also stretch from side to side, in which case you drop your head with the ear toward either shoulder, being careful not to drop the head forward. Go down the neck, through the shoulder girdle, down the ribs, and down the lower back to the pelvis.

As you sit on your horse, consider what you have been doing up to this point. You have learned about the various parts of your anatomy, what they look like and how they feel. You have become more aware of your body. Now I want you to search your mind for the interrelationship of all these parts. You already know how the lower back, pelvis, and hip joint affect each other; and how the curves of the spine and balance of the head depend on each other. Increasingly you will discover other interrelationships. For instance, if you tighten your jaw, it will affect the whole spine and body. If you wiggle your toes and allow your feet to feel wide and flat on the stirrups, you'll be able to soften your spine and neck. If your shoulders are tight, your breathing will be shallow. Think of what happens with a tensed neck or buttocks, and so on. There is no end, for each part of the body in some way, great or small, affects every other part.

I want to mention again the special importance of freedom and balance in the head and neck. The Alexander Technique is based on what F. M. Alexander called primary control: Let the neck be free to let the head go forward and up and to let the back be long and wide. Notice in each case you must "let," not "make," anything happen. To let the neck be free you don't wiggle it around—that's *doing* something. Rather you must allow it to feel soft and empty. To let the head go properly forward and up, you should look straight ahead with your soft eyes and then imagine the tug of some hair pulled up from the top of your head. (See Fig. 39.)

This combination will result in energy moving diagonally forward and up from the tip of your forehead. The head is not pushed in that direction, only the energy flows that way. As the back is allowed to be wide through the shoulders, across the shoulder blades and diaphragm, the lower back and hips will also be able to lengthen. The sacrum will then be free to drop and make the pelvis level.

At this point the body is free and balanced and available for any riding activity. For example, by freeing your neck and head you will be able to soften your hip joint and lengthen your leg.

Alexander found that one of the most pervasive physical problems in our Western culture is tension of the neck, perhaps due to the stresses of modern living. How many times in your daily life, as well as in your riding, do you tense your neck as you do something? Getting out of a chair, writing, peeling carrots in a hurry, or even thinking hard about something, can all tighten you up. The Alexander Technique teaches you to become aware of your body and its problems. Then you can learn to inhibit the problems. When you practice this, if your neck is the difficulty, feel as if it were empty and free as you walk off on your horse and allow your body to move without that upper tension.

Allow yourself to accept the new sensations. Use imagery instead of force, then wait for the natural movements to take over. *Become aware. Inhibit. Allow.* These are the keys. A teacher can be a tremendous help in the first two phases. But the allowing can only come from you.

While the overall process is subtle, and not very dramatic, the results can be both tremendous and exhilarating.

Increased body awareness gives you a greater awareness of your inner self as well as your surroundings. Changing your habits will cultivate an ability to make clearer choices: A balanced body permits a balanced state of mind.

*What are the essentials of knowing anatomy?*
- Ride your bones.
- Become aware of your hip joints.
- Let your legs hang from your hip joints like flippers.
- Hang your leg like an old gate on one hinge.
- Leave your lower back hanging long and soft.

- Keep your lower legs like weights on a string.
- Imagine pulling the strings on your ankles.
- Feel your shoulder girdle like a yoke.
- Grow your collarbones.
- Soften your neck and balance your head.
- Be aware of the interrelationship of all parts of your body.
- Pull straight up on some hair directly on top of your head, like a puppet hanging on string.

## What are the results of knowing anatomy?

- Increased body awareness.
- Changing your old habits and cultivating your ability to make clearer choices.
- Your balanced body will create a balanced state of mind.

# 6

# Balance and Body Freedom

In order to be a successful centered rider, your torso must be laterally balanced. Ask a friend or instructor to watch from behind as you walk away in a straight line without stirrups—legs hanging free and limp—and then walk back. One half of the people I teach do not sit squarely; they sit between one-quarter inch to two inches off center. (Figs. 47 & 48.) This unevenness is very evident from behind, because the line of the spine and the back seam of the pants do not come over the horse's backbone. These lines may come over the middle of the saddle, but then the saddle may be pulled to one side also. The rider's feet are not level as they hang.

For many people the right leg is stronger than the left, but whichever leg is stronger, that whole side of the body tends to be shorter than the other side. If you have a stronger right leg, you will swing your pelvis over to the right as you go up in the rising trot. This also causes your right seat bone to carry more weight. As a result you will find that you cannot feel your left seat bone and that your left leg feels too short. In making an effort to correct these feelings you constantly reach down with your left leg, which pulls the saddle and your pelvis over to the left side.

In order to sit squarely on your horse, you will need a person on the ground to help you find your true lateral balance. As this person watches you from behind, step heavily on your right stirrup to pull the saddle back onto the center of your horse's back. Then have your helper tell you when you are sitting evenly on the saddle. Now you will feel very strange and awful—as if you were falling off to the right.

But you are not! You are now even. You must face the realization that the old familiar feeling was incorrect, and that this new and terrible sensation is the way you should

47. *Sitting off center.*

48. *Sitting squarely.*

51

feel! Furthermore, you must memorize this new feeling because you will need it in all your future riding.

Various exercises are available to help you keep your correct balance. Let us still assume that you have a stronger right leg, so as you walk without stirrups put your right arm straight up over your head and imagine the fingers growing up to the sky. This will release and lengthen your right side and leg, and you will feel more secure.

Keep walking with soft eyes, and test your memory of this new feeling by wiggling around, upsetting your balance, and then find the new position again. Then put your feet in your stirrups and pick up the rising trot. Check to see which leg and foot is carrying more weight. You can find this out by changing your diagonal at the trot every few strides without changing direction.

You will find your right foot carrying more weight than the left. So imagine that you siphon (Fig. 49) the weight out of your heavy, strong leg and drop it into the light, weak leg. The weak leg may tire as it takes on its full share of the load, but it will become strong if you persist. The soles of your feet should feel alike. Spread out your toes in your boots to help the evenness.

For those of you who are unclear about diagonals, I shall explain: In the trot, a two-beat gait, the horse's legs move in alternate diagonal pairs. When you are rising to the trot, your seat is in the saddle on one beat and above it on the other. If you sit when the horse's left front foot and right hind foot strike the ground, you are rising on the left diagonal. In circling right it is correct for you to be on the left diagonal and vice versa. To change diagonals you sit two beats of the trot or stay in the air for two beats.

It helps to have someone check you periodically as you walk without stirrups to be sure you are correct. If you are tired or haven't ridden for a few weeks, the old one-sided habits can come back. It is a good idea, each time you get on a horse, to check your evenness with a few changes of diagonals at the posting trot. This is critical in the development of a balanced rider and horse.

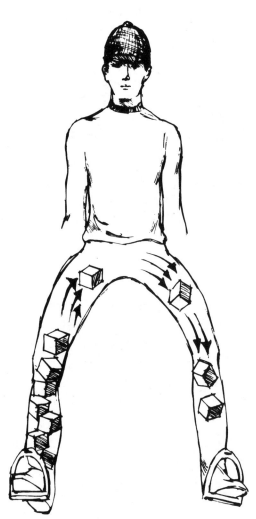

49. *Siphon some weight out of the heavy leg and drop it into the light one.*

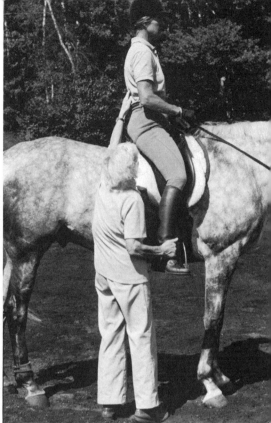

50. *The helper placing the fingers of one hand over the spine at the bottom of the rider's rib cage.*

You may have another balance problem. You could tend to sit with your torso tipped a bit too forward or back and cannot find the feeling of true upright balance. Try leaning your torso first definitely too far forward and then too far back. Notice that in each case you need your legs to hold you on, which means tightening your hip joints and thigh muscles. Now pretend your legs have been cut off at the hip joints. Put as much of your seat on the saddle as possible and find where you can balance your body without using any legs at all. In this way, you can achieve correct upright balance without someone else around to check you.

To discover the sensations of allowing your body and legs to lengthen, you will need a helper on the ground. When you sit without stirrups, you are asking your horse to stand squarely on all four feet. Rethink the Alexander Technique instructions—free the neck to allow the head to balance forward and up and to allow the back to be long and wide. Free your neck simply, by making it feel empty, not cranking it around. Find the balance of your head as explained in Chapter 5.

Ask your helper to put his hand on your back with his fingers over your spine at the bottom of your rib cage. (Fig. 50.) Give yourself time to feel your back radiate from this spot, up through your neck and head as it also broadens and lengthens downward. Now ask your helper to hold his fingertips on the same spot, the bottom of the rib cage. Imagine a line of energy streaming up from his fingertips through your body, forward and up, out through the top of your sternum (breastbone) into the sky. (Fig. 51.) You must not push it. Let it flow through you effortlessly like a laser beam. Imagine a similar beam running from the top of your sternum, backward, and up, out through the nape of your neck. These two diagonal streams of energy will make your upper body feel light, as if suspended in a hammock.

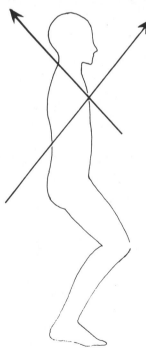

51. *Diagonal streams of energy.*

53

52. *Lowering the sacrum onto the ground.*

53. *Position of the helper to initially draw the leg back.*

Keeping that suspended feeling, ask your helper to touch your sacrum (the part of your spine that goes through the back of your pelvis), and then put his fingertips at the bottom of your rib cage. Now imagine that the fingertips are holding a string just inside your body that is attached to your sacrum. (Fig. 52.) Let the sacrum, in your imagination, drop down on that string through the saddle, through your horse's body, out his belly, and on down to the ground, where it will gently rest. You will find that in doing this your lower back, hip joints, and legs have appreciably softened and relaxed.

Next ask your helper to stand beside your horse, behind the saddle and facing forward. With his near hand to the horse he should gently take hold of your ankle and draw your whole leg from the hip joint, softly back as far as it will come without strain. (Fig. 53.) It is important that he use his hand near the horse as that helps to rotate the outside of the leg forward. (Figs. 54a & b.) Pulling too hard against resisting muscles can cause damage. Let him hold your leg in that position while you explore your body, especially the upper body, to see what tensions can be released. Soften your neck under your ear, under your armpit, and behind your sternum. Keep your soft eyes, center yourself, and breathe. You will find the pull of your leg in your helper's hand will have decreased. He can now take it back another bit without strain. Yet even with your leg long and that far back, farther than you will ever need it, your buttock sits soft and relaxed on the saddle and your body is at ease.

Now ask your helper to stand at your knee facing the horse's tail. (Fig. 55.) Let him take your whole leg back to a suitable position for an outside aid. He can then lightly support your toe with his hand nearest the horse and lay the other hand over the back of your ankle. Feel that your foot is sinking toward your horse's hind foot with the quality of a stone sinking through water. You don't push the stone down. You just release it. Free your neck and upper body as you did before, center yourself, and breathe. You will mysteriously feel your leg and heel sink all on their own, not helped by you. Notice, too, that because of the releases at the hip, your foot hangs nearly parallel to the horse's body—no toe sticking out. What a super outside aid!

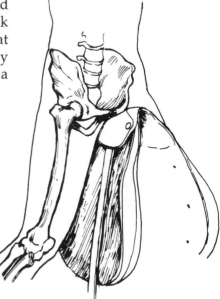

54a & b. The position of the bones with the leg in correct normal position and then the correct position drawn back. Note how the greater trochanter rotates forward when the leg is drawn back.

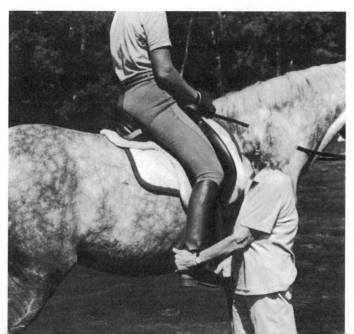

55. Position for asking the rider to allow her own leg and heel to drop back toward the horse's hind foot, as if for an outside aid.

56. *Position for asking the rider to drop leg straight down, as if for an inside aid.*

57. *This is the starting point for the energy diagonal that travels up and out the top of your sternum.*

Lastly, ask your helper to stand facing you, again with one hand lightly under your toe and the other at your ankle. (Fig. 56.) This time allow your leg to sink straight down, as if for an inside aid. Center and breathe, free your neck, armpit, and behind your sternum. In your imagination cut your leg off at your hip, cast off those strings attaching it to your upper body, and let it drop. It is nearly one-quarter of your weight and will hit the ground with a thump! Your leg might drop an inch or more with this technique, and certainly it will soften and lengthen. Done repeatedly in your horse's rhythm at any gait, it becomes the basis for the perfect inside aid.

Through all these simple exercises you have found a way to achieve extraordinary results in softening, lengthening, and using your body—not by doing anything, but by using imagery and allowing freedom. These exercises are explained from an instructor's point of view in Appendix II on page 187.

Once you have learned how to achieve these new sensations with the aid of your helper, you can free your body and legs without him by using a quick routine that I call "Being an Indian." Sitting on your horse without stirrups, put the back of your hand on your back where your helper did, and use it as the focal point from which to feel your body lengthen and widen and to sense the upward energy lines lighten your upper torso while your lower back and sacrum drop. (Fig. 57.)

The next step is to pretend you are the Indian whose statue stands outside the Museum of Fine Arts in Boston. (Fig. 58.) He sits balanced, legs long, his back straight and not arched, looking up and out as he worships the Great Spirit. His arms hang outward, with the palms of his hands facing in the same direction as his eyes. Now you sit in this same position and allow yourself to find the feeling of upward openness so apparent in the statue. Give yourself time to really release. Feel yourself growing down as well as up, and being open.

Finish the Indian routine by sitting quietly with your hand on your lower belly, contemplating your center— that deep area of power and energy. At the end of this exercise, you will find that your hips and legs are totally free, just as if your legs were lengthened by your helper.

*What are the essentials of balance and body freedom?*
- Use your Four Basics.
- Be sure you are sitting evenly.
- Remember the leg-lengthening experience.
- Imagine being the Indian in *Appeal to the Great Spirit*. (Fig. 58.)

*What are the results of balance and body freedom?*
- Better sense of balance.
- Awareness of the need to soften and balance your neck and head in order to release the lower back and hips.

58. *Cyrus E. Dallin's statue, Appeal to the Great Spirit. Allow yourself to sit this way, feeling long, upward, and outward. (Photo: Courtesy, Museum of Fine Arts, Boston. Gift of Peter C. Brooks and others.)*

# 7

# Walk and the Following Seat

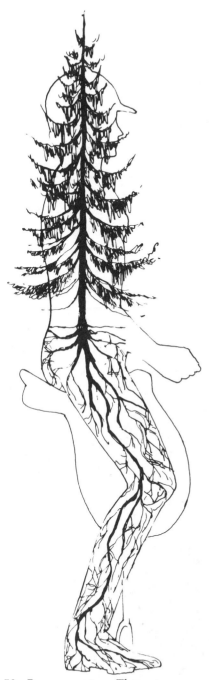

The walk is a four-beat gait—you can hear each foot separately touch the ground with every complete stride. The horse at all times has three feet on the ground. His body is never in suspension. Each individual foot affects his back, with the result that the saddle is tipped around more than at any other gait. At the trot the saddle goes only up and down, and at the canter it swings somewhat like a rocking chair. But at the walk it is tilted around in all directions.

To follow the horse's back at the walk, you must have a deep, mobile receiving seat. Your balance and mobility can directly affect the quality of your horse's walk. A horse with a natural long, swinging stride at a walk has an asset that must be nurtured and treasured. A horse with a stilted, short, or shambling walk can be improved, but only by a rider who has the correct techniques. Because you can learn so much at the walk, we shall do many exercises in that gait. What you learn there will carry over easily into the trot and canter.

This is a good time to imagine, while you walk your horse without stirrups, that you are a spruce tree with your branches hanging down. The trunk of the tree goes up from your center through your torso, all the way up between your ears and out the top of your head. (Fig. 59.) The branches hang. Your jaw hangs from under your ears. Your arms and shoulders hang from your head and neck. Your ribs hang from your spine and sternum. All the branches are free to sway in the breeze. The trunk also is not rigid. It can sway, but never collapses. Your center and pelvis are the mulch at the ground line, and your legs are the roots. As the trunk of the tree grows up, the roots grow down deeper and deeper to balance it. But the tree can't *make* itself grow. It just grows. You should allow your body to extend upward from your center as your legs grow down around your horse from that same place. It takes very soft eyes to grow well.

59. *Be a spruce tree. The roots grow down from your center as the trunk grows up.*

60. *Imagine that your legs have been cut off just above the knee and you are riding with thighs only.*

Now try something different. Stretch your body tall—really force it up there. What happened to the relationship between your seat and the saddle? Your seat went up and off the saddle. Next, stop stretching and go back to growing. How does your seat feel now? It should be heavier, wider, and deeper, spreading all over the saddle.

With your body and hips freely balanced, it will be easy to follow the horse's motion. Try this other exercise to improve your seat at the walk. Sit on the middle of your seat bones and pretend that both your legs have been cut off just above your knees. (Fig. 60.) Imagine that you have no legs below your lower thighs. Notice that this image immediately causes your thighs to soften and drop. Most people think of their legs from the knees down and this causes strain in their thighs. My students have found that this image of having stubby short legs has helped them forget their lower legs altogether. Some say "How do you stay on without your lower legs?" It can be done. A student told me that she had once gone trail-riding with a double amputee whose legs did not come even halfway to his knees. Considering he wore no harness, what depth of centering, balance, and suppleness he must have had!

To remain stable you must keep as much contact as possible; but it must be fluid, or you could be bounced from your horse's back and might or might not come down in the same place. In short, your pelvis must move in complete, relaxed contact with the horse's back. Make the most efficient use of your stubby legs. If you roll your thighs back and/or tighten your buttocks, you will tend to go up and off your horse. If you depend on squeezing with your legs, you will do the same. If, on the other hand, you let the outer top of your femurs (thigh bones) rotate forward, as you did when your leg was pulled, you will find that you become quite stable.

The inside fronts of your stubby legs will fall over the stirrup bars (the clips onto which the stirrup leathers are hooked) and down the sides of your saddle in front of the stirrup leathers. This will make the top three or four inches of your thighs fill the saddle over the stirrup bars, close to, and on either side of, the pommel. Once this rotation of the femurs is achieved without altering the level or angle of the pelvis, you will find you have the well-known three-point seat—seat bones and crotch— without the discomfort of a sore or squashed crotch against the pommel. The relaxed upper front of the thighs provide a solid cushion on either side of the pommel, giving the desired crotch contact. Furthermore, you now have a close seat that is not the product of any muscular tension, but solely due to the placement of your pelvis and stubby legs.

As you acquire this seat, another very important thing happens. Until now, when you sat on the middle of your seat bones, most of your body weight was on them and the buttocks. As you develop the concept of stubby legs and learn to place them in the correct forward position, thinking of your tree growth, you will become conscious of the fact that within your body you have redistributed your weight. It is no longer only on your seat bones and buttocks. Quite a lot of the weight is now dripping down over the stirrup bars—and your pelvis still remains level.

Now you have progressed from two little spots of weight on the horse's back to offering him, instead, a wide band of weight, emanating from buttocks, seat bones, and thighs. (Fig. 61.)

This distribution is vastly preferable to the horse. The horse's spine, through the withers (at the shoulder), has very little motion. From there to the loin, the possibilities for swing and motion in the spine increase. So from the horse's point of view, and from yours also, the farther forward you sit on his back, the more comfortable it is for him and the more stable it is for you.

The horse's center of gravity lies between the stirrup leathers, an inch or two below the saddle flaps; it varies a little forward or back with his activity. In the galloping and jumping positions, the rider's weight is largely or totally carried on the stirrups and is therefore automatically over the horse's center of gravity. Owing to the springiness of your hips, knees, and ankles, it is a soft seat, most of the time close to but not actually on the saddle. When you work on the flat, however, you want the extra control and finesse that comes from the greatest possible contact. Through the use of the three-point seat—seat bones, buttocks, and stubby legs—not only can you remain soft while working on the flat, but you will be as near as possible to your horse's center of gravity.

Now walk your horse without stirrups. Just center yourself, and feel and hear the four beats of the walk. Then begin to allow your buttocks to follow the hind feet. When the horse's right hind foot comes forward and starts to push back, the belly will swing over it. As he puts weight on that foot, his back will rise and lift your right buttock. As his hind leg stretches back and starts forward again, the horse's back will drop, taking your right buttock with it. Pay attention to one buttock at a time as you feel each one lift and drop. Allow the horse to do it to you. This is important in learning to listen to your horse with your body. It refines your awareness of the pulsations of the horse's back and also the exact position and movement of the horse's hind legs. Feel these pulsations ripple up through your body, shoulders, neck, and head, like the

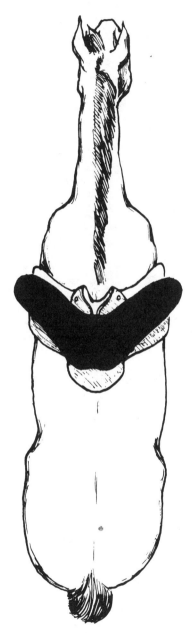

61. A wide band of weight covering the horse's back, seen from above.

61

*62. With your arm over your head, point your fingers to the sky.*

ripples you see after you have dropped a pebble in a pond.

Notice the constant motion in your hip joints caused by the rise and fall of the stubby legs following the horse's shoulders. Feel around for this, first left side, then right side, as you did with the buttocks. You'll find you can receive and synchronize the lift and fall—one, two, three, four—buttock, leg, buttock, leg. Now you are very quiet in the saddle and can have a feeling of sharing a common skin between your seat and the horse's back, instead of forcing yourself to move excessively.

An exercise that will help you find these receiving sensations is to ride with one hand stretched over your head. (Fig. 62.) Stretch one arm straight up and keep your fingers pointing and growing toward the sky while the rest of the body drops below. (This, by the way, is a great technique for unlocking and loosening the lower back and hip joints at any gait.) Either hand will do. Change hands whenever you get tired. With hand high over your head, become aware of the feeling of elasticity up and down the front of your body. Try to keep the same sensations of balance and freedom as you bring your hand down to the normal position. Your body, neck, and head should feel tall and quiet, and your seat soft, receptive, and moving.

Some of my students become so infatuated with this exercise that I often wonder if I'll ever get them to ride with two hands again. Once, I had a student who announced that at her next competition she was going to go out behind the barn and do nothing else but warm up with one hand over her head.

With your new awareness, notice at the walk that your stubby leg drops at the same moment your buttock rises. Directly after this, the horse moves your seat bone slightly forward. The sequence of motion is: stubby leg drop, seat bone slides forward, again leg drop, slide forward, and so on. Your leg comes down when the horse's hind leg, on the same side, takes weight; the seat bone slides when his opposite leg takes weight. If you *let* your horse move your seat bone, giving it to him generously, he will walk freely. But if you lock your hips, not allowing that slide, he will slow down or even stop. At the other extreme, if you *drive* him forward with the seat bone, he will go—but with resistance and tension.

Now let's see if you can produce varying lengths of stride in your horse's walk, with your seat alone. Avoid using any leg aid. For the moment ride with long reins and no contact with the horse's mouth. In a really free walk the horse will use his whole body, his belly swinging sideways with each step and his head and neck moving up and down as well as somewhat sideways. There is a fine line between allowing your horse to slide your seat bone and your pushing. Try not to push. A generous slide will enhance your soft receiving and following seat. You will feel your horse expand his stride, reaching his hind feet well forward with each swinging step. The overstep— the distance the hind foot steps beyond the front foot—

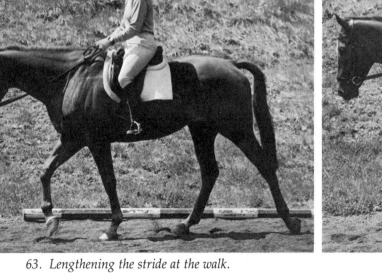

63. *Lengthening the stride at the walk.*          64. *Shortening the stride at the walk.*

will markedly increase. His back and neck will stretch and have greater motion. (Fig. 63.) You'll become aware of his forward surge of energy as he fills your seat.

To shorten the stride, simply reduce your activity. Do not become rigid, just less active. Control your suppleness, reduce the amount you allow your seat bone to slide, but do not lose the upward pulsations or hold your breath. (Fig. 64.) As you alternate between generously sliding seat bones and reduced activity, you should be able to vary your horse's stride by as much as six inches—and remember, this is without using any lower legs or reins. If you then start to do this exercise with light rein contact, you will feel that you are walking the horse's hind feet up toward the front end, not pulling the front end back.

If, by chance, your horse gets lazy about listening to your seat, flick him with your whip or wake him up with a positive kick from your legs. Then go back to receiving and giving, and he will hear you.

An important benefit of this exercise is that when riding with stirrups, the alternating motion of the sliding seat bone and stubby-leg drop causes the stubby leg to press the side of your calves against the horse, behind his girth and below the saddle. It requires a soft knee and ankle to do this, and once achieved will create a rhythmical and correct use of your lower leg.

The ability to feel, receive, and follow the upward pulsation of the horse's back is crucial not only at the walk, but also at the trot and canter. The horse feels a new freedom to use his back. At any gait, if you stiffen a portion of your seat, the horse's stride will become less fluid and powerful. The more you sense and receive the upbeats of his strides through the buttocks, the better the horse's back will fill your seat. His strides become more elastic and powerful, and the purity of the gait is improved. With this sensitive seat, you can address your horse in a very precise manner.

Riding this way is like playing a finely tuned instrument, at times delicate, at other times powerful. Imagine a grand piano settled deep in your pelvis. (See Fig. 133.) The true artist can play with equal dexterity a soft ballad or a crashing march.

## What are the essentials of the walk and following seat?

- Use your Four Basics.
- Find your three-point seat: seat bones, buttocks, and the top three inches of the inside fronts of your thighs.
- Hear, feel, and receive the pulsations, rhythm, and motion of the stride.
- Use your images: spruce tree, energy diagonals, stubby legs, and hand over head.
- Feel that you share a common skin with your horse, so that your seat follows the horse's back.
- Allow your seat bone to slide every stride.
- Allow yourself and your horse's back to swing in rhythm.

## What are the results of the walk and following seat?

- Awareness of your horse's movement.
- Better sense of receptivity.
- More subtle control over the horse's movement.
- Your horse can use his whole body better.
- The rhythm and purity of the stride improves.

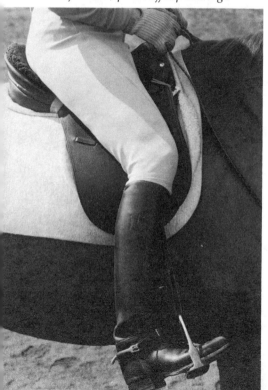

65a. *Correct leg, not pushing on the stirrup.*

b. *Incorrect leg, pushing on the stirrup, with the lower leg thrust forward, plus stiff hip and leg.*

# 8

# Rising (Posting) Trot

**B**efore you trot, think about your stirrups. They are there to rest on, not to push on. They are there to carry the weight of your legs, not the whole body. Try pushing on your stirrups and note the stiffening that goes up through your body. (Figs. 65a–c.) Now relax again and let the stirrups carry just your legs. Move into a rising trot—a nice, comfortable, unhurried trot—using the whole arena, letting your stirrups support your whole weight. Remember your building blocks and, keeping your eyes soft, let your shoulders balance erect above your pelvis and stirrups. Let all the weight drop through your body right

c. *Incorrect leg in the rising trot, showing tension through rider's entire body, head to toe. Horse is tending to draw back his neck and head; notice also that the ears are back.*

down and through your stirrups. Don't block your weight at the hips, knees, or ankles. (Figs. 66a & b.) Don't pinch the saddle with your thighs, knees, or calves. The horse will be uncomfortable if you squeeze too much and will not move freely.

With every rise, let your pelvis come forward and up as if you were being pulled gently by the belt buckle. (See Fig. 19.) Think forward—that is, see and feel forward-moving energy—and keep your legs long and closed gently against your horse's sides. Let your body melt like ice cream and dribble down into and out the bottom of your boots. (Fig. 67.)

With soft eyes, organize your breathing. Center yourself and feel your center of gravity drop through your belt line— *plunk!*—down into your boots along with the ice cream. Keep trotting and think more about your breathing. Let the bellows open and shut rhythmically so that the air flows in and out through your whole body. Keep reminding yourself of the bellows. (See Fig. 9.) It is important that breathing, as well as centering and soft eyes, remain constant through all your riding.

*66a. Soft knee not pinching. Lower leg lies on horse's side.*

*b. Pinched knee. Lower leg is pushed out and thigh and hip are stiff.*

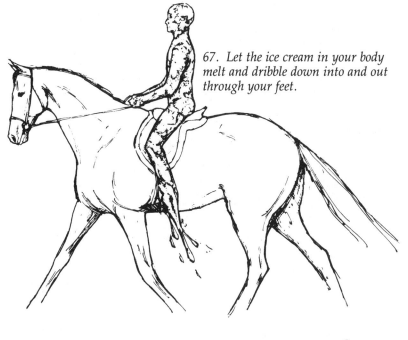

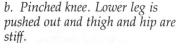

*67. Let the ice cream in your body melt and dribble down into and out through your feet.*

*68a & b. Balanced rider at the posting trot, up and down.*

*c. Unbalanced rider, causing resistance and discomfort in the horse.*

Begin to search for the rhythm of the horse. His energy and rhythm come from his hind legs. You should feel them doing the work, while the front legs go along for the ride. You push a wheelbarrow from behind and the wheel in front goes forward, but the energy comes from behind. Build up to a positive and steady one-two-one-two sound. You will find that you cannot ask your horse to obey your aids until you are in tune with whatever rhythm he is giving you, even if it is an incorrect rhythm, one that is too rapid or irregular.

Listen and be aware of those hind legs. Feel the rhythm come up through your body and feel your center going with the upward pulsations as the push of his inside hind foot thrusts your buttock up. Try to feel that the weight on your stirrups is the same whether you are going up or down. This means that you will touch the saddle very lightly as you come down. Be aware of how much your hip and knee joints open and close as you post. Your knees must move as freely as your hips. Use all the joints fully. (Figs. 68a–c.)

Still trotting, think about your feet. You will probably now find that they are more directly beneath you than they were before. Seen from the side, your ear, shoulder, hip, and ankle will now line up. Are you even on your two stirrups? Spread all your toes out inside your boots and let the whole width of the foot carry your weight on the stirrups. (Figs. 69a & b.) The weight on the big toe should be equal to the weight on the little toe. Your feet should feel the same on the stirrups.

It's also important not to neglect your ankles. Stiffening your ankles tenses your entire body almost as much as setting your jaw does. How can you learn to have soft ankles? First, try shaking your wrist and forearm as if you were going to shake the fingers right off your hand. Notice that the fingers become very soft. If you then stiffen your fingers, you'll find you can no longer shake a loose hand. The same is true with your foot. Try it. You cannot shake your foot with tense toes. Soft, free toes are essential to free the ankles. Place your foot flat on the stirrup and pretend to play scales lightly on the piano with your toes. Do this until you feel equal weight on all of your toes. Now your ankle can be soft.

Riders are often told to turn their foot in, making it parallel to the horse. If this is done with conscious effort, the ankle, leg, and hip will tense up, and your weight will be on the outside edge of your foot. If, however, your leg is hung correctly from a well-balanced body and pelvis, the foot will hang softly, very nearly parallel to the horse's side.

How often do you hear "Drive your heels down!"? Unfortunately, forcing the heels down can only stiffen you and lift you out of the saddle. Since your legs are heavy anyway (each one perhaps 25 percent of your weight), why not give them over to gravity? Gravity will drop your *soft* ankles and heels down—lower than you can push them.

Remember, though, your heel can only drop as far as your Achilles tendon will let it. Tendons stretch very little, even with long practice. If you have short Achilles tendons, you will never have deep heels. Don't worry. Live

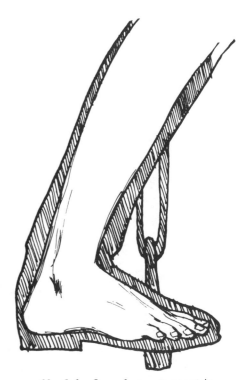

*69a & b. Spread your toes out inside your boots. Some people tend to clench them.*

with them wherever gravity takes them, provided you keep your ankles free and soft. Remember also that for your ankles to be soft, they must hang below, not in front of, your hip joints. Forward feet will result in stiff ankles. Soft ankles will allow the heels to sink with each posting motion of the trot.

If you find you are behind the motion of the horse—your center behind your feet—imagine a string attached to the top of your forehead pulling you forward and up, and visualize your body as a floppy dishrag being dragged through water by the string. You, the rag, trail helplessly along behind the string. And you will find yourself synchronized again with the horse's motion.

If you still have trouble maintaining your balance or keeping your feet beneath you while posting, try the following exercise: Have a helper lead or lunge your horse as you ride. At the halt, stand straight up on your stirrups and bring your pelvis forward, over, and in front of the pommel. Keep your heels back and fully depressed. You should not be sitting on the pommel. As you balance in front of the pommel with your heels back and down, allow the front of your thighs to press against the front of the saddle flaps. The pressure between your weighted heels with relaxed ankles and your supported thighs will make your upper body stable. As a result, you can fully open the front of your hip joint, leave your pelvis level, and keep your torso up and arched slightly forward. Do not hollow your lower back. Be careful not to hold on by pinching with your knees; this will stiffen you, and you'll lose the benefits of the exercise by not truly balancing yourself. Carry your head high and somewhat back, with your eyes looking straight ahead. Stretch your arms out sideways, palms up. (Fig. 70.)

Now your helper can progress at a walk. If you keep your center of gravity down, breathe evenly, and have your heels well down, your arched body will feel open and secure when your horse moves. As you become accustomed to the motion, try moving your arms up and around in all directions. It is a good exercise to gain the feeling of freedom and openness in the front of the body

70. *Balancing in front of the saddle to learn that you can feel stable with your feet well back.*

and hip joints. You will also find a sense of security in a low center of gravity and the support provided by the front of the saddle's sides. You'll be surprised how far back your feet can be and still hold you balanced. This can also be done on the lunge line with side reins—at the trot and the canter as well.

Now resume your normal position in the saddle and you'll see that you do not need to brace your feet forward at the rising trot. As you are moving along, imagine that you're wearing a shirt with many buttons. Let the buttons come undone, one by one. Starting from the neck, open the shirt out to the sides and allow the front of your body to come through. We spend too much of our lives working over a desk or bench or sink with our chests pulled together and tied with a double-bow knot at the front and bottom of the ribs. (Fig. 71.) Undo all these knots and open the front of the body. Allow half of your torso to be in front of your arms. You want your horse to move with big, open strides and a light carriage. Since you are at the controls, you are the leader when you ask your horse to perform. Your body, therefore, must be free to lead.

71. *We spend too much of our lives being tense and tied up with a double-bow knot.*

71

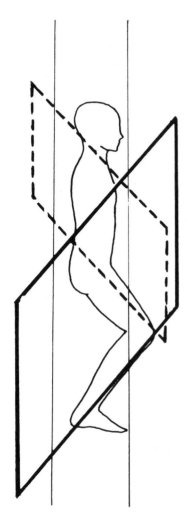

*72. Riding within parallelograms—formed by the perpendicular lines of the building blocks, crossed by the energy lines through the upper body and the angles of the thigh and lower leg.*

When doing this exercise, it helps to invoke the diagonal-lines image discussed earlier. (See Fig. 51.) This image can be expanded as follows. A little thought and observation of other riders will show that the line of the rider's lower leg should be parallel to the diagonal line that goes forward and up from the back through the sternum. (Fig. 72.) These diagonal lines, when combined with the vertical lines of your building blocks, form a parallelogram. If the lower leg moves too far forward, the balance of the parallelogram is lost. Correct balance and a feeling of security comes from imagining yourself riding within the correct lines of the parallelogram.

A second parallelogram can be made by visualizing the energy diagonal that travels from the top of the sternum back and up, through the nape of the neck. Extend this diagonal down and it will be parallel to the line of your thigh. Many riders use the first parallelogram in their imagery more than the second one, but for a rider with a tendency to carry the head and/or shoulders forward, the second one is of great importance.

The feeling of stability acquired by riding within the parallelograms can be enhanced by imagining that your legs are growing longer, so long that your feet are resting flat on the ground—ground that is soft, warm summer mud. (Fig. 73.) Let it ooze up between your relaxed toes; enjoy the warmth around your feet and ankles. The pleasure of letting your feet down into the mud has the effect of softening the legs, knees, and ankles. Your seat will deepen in the saddle while lengthening, quieting and stabilizing the lower legs and feet. Any pinching by the knees will disappear.

There are substantial benefits from riding with these images of parallelograms and feet in the mud. The lower leg will move back and stay under the rider. The upper body will feel secure in its attachment to the center and, at the same time, will develop lightness and independence through the upward energy of the diagonals. The shoulder joint becomes independent, so the arms and hand become very quiet and sensitive.

73. *Imagine that your legs are so long that your feet rest on the ground; here's when you can wiggle your toes in the warm mud.*

The resulting reaction of the horse is a joy to feel. You have been released from many tensions, causing the horse to feel released as well. His eyes and ears become relaxed and contented. His back relaxes, too, and fills the rider's seat. He reaches out and down for the bit. If you just think about a longer stride from the horse's inside hind leg, the strides will inevitably become longer and more flowing, and his back begins to swing softly. It is a picture of great harmony between horse and rider, showing fluid, energetic forward motion.

Think once more about your horse. If your center is between your diaphragm and pelvis, so is your horse's center of control between his diaphragm and pelvis. It is behind and below your center, approximately eighteen inches away. When you trot again, think about putting those two centers together. Use your awareness and imagination to sense the strength and the rhythm coming up from the horse's hind legs through his center and your center, out through the horse's withers, neck, and poll (at the top of the head). Keep that energy surging up rhythmically from behind and out through you.

You have been doing a posting trot using the whole ring. Now prepare for doing twenty-meter circles here and there—at the ends of the ring as well as at the center. Before you start your circle, prepare yourself. Organize your breathing, center yourself, and quietly create the bend that starts from behind, going forward from the horse's inside hind leg. Keep your outside leg farther back on his side in order to control his hindquarters giving him support, and use your inside leg, as needed, to maintain a rhythmic forward energy and tempo.

Now think of your horse's hind legs again. With soft use of your inside leg near the girth, feel his inside hind foot come farther under you with each stride and feel the strides get longer. (Fig. 74.) Don't increase the speed, just let the strides lengthen. Keep breathing, keep centering. To help the horse lengthen his stride, make the thrust of your rise more positive—not necessarily higher—from the front of your lower spine, behind your belt buckle. His shoulders will automatically swing with the longer strides, but the thrust must come from behind and flow out through the withers into your quiet hands.

I can hear you saying it now: "It's so easy! I *feel* more with my horse. When I come down on his back, it's softer. The saddle isn't just a place to bounce from. I feel more even distribution of contact with my seat, thighs, knees, and stirrups. It's as if I'm fitting over him like a soft glove. My horse is going better without my telling him."

Bravo! These are good thoughts and feelings. You should talk about them with your instructor and fellow students to further establish the images in your right brain. It is no wonder your horse is going better. You are no longer behind his center of gravity. Do you remember, much earlier on, how relieved you were, on your hands and knees, when your friend stopped poking you so hard on your back? In the same way, your horse appreciates the freedom from your bouncing seat bones. If he was nervous and in a hurry earlier, he is probably quiet now, with a lower head and neck. If he had a tendency to be lazy, he is now more willing to move forward. His strides are long, swinging, and rhythmical. You and your horse have a new relationship: You are a happy horse-person.

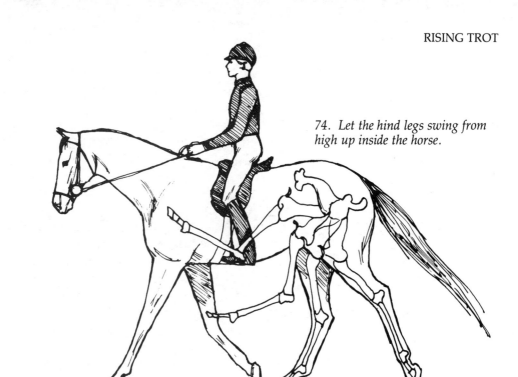

*74. Let the hind legs swing from high up inside the horse.*

## *What are the essentials of a correct rising trot?*

- Use your Four Basics.
- Let your weight go down through your stirrups without pinching or blocking.
- Keep your weight distributed evenly between your stirrups.
- Drag the dishrag (your body) through the water.
- Use your knee and hip joints freely.
- Keep a steady rhythm coming from behind.
- Open your imaginary shirt.
- Lead the horse from your center.
- Ride within your parallelograms.
- Ride with your feet in the mud.

## *What are the results of a correct rising trot?*

- Balance with your horse.
- Rhythm with your horse.
- Energy is built in the trot.
- Horse moves forward more freely and steadily.

# 9

# Hands

Quiet, sensitive hands are important in all aspects of riding. Your arms and hands, from the shoulder joints to the tips of the fingers and through the reins, belong to the horse. He directs the movement of your hands, and the level of his head determines the level of your hands. Your back, seat, and legs control the horse's hindquarters, and the arms and hands control the forehand. Synchronized, they direct the energy of the entire horse.

All major motion of the horse's head will be absorbed by your shoulders and elbows. Noted dressage trainer and author Charles deKunffy says that God created riders with the wrong conformation. A rider's forearm should be long enough to extend from the elbow to the bit so you could hook your fingers in the bit, or better yet, over the corners of the horse's mouth. (Fig. 75.) Then you'd really have a sensitive and direct feel! You can, however, be sensitive even with the use of reins. Many small and subtle indications to the horse come solely through your fingers and hands.

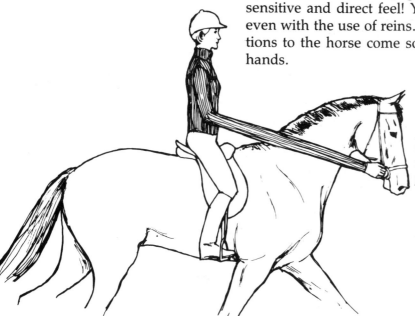

75. *Charles deKunffy says that if God had given us conformation for riding, our forearms would reach from elbow to bit.*

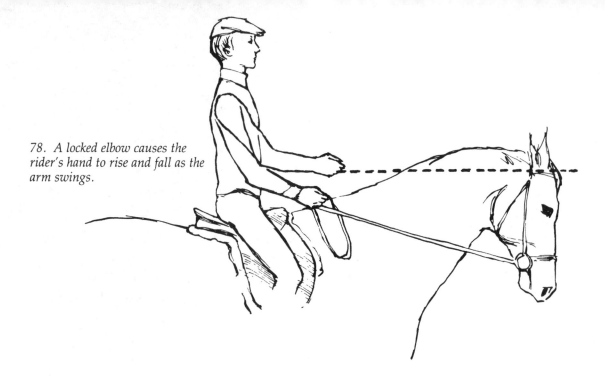

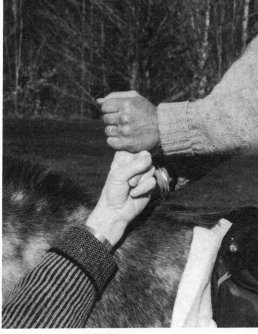

Good hands are profoundly dependent on a good seat, one that is soft and deep. Unless the motion of the horse is largely absorbed by your hip joints, knees, and ankles, your shoulders will jump and your head will bob. When this is the case, the rough motion will be reflected in your unsteady hands. "No seat, no hands" is a true statement!

I'm sure you are familiar with this problem of not being able to keep your hands steady, thereby producing a jerky motion on the horse's mouth. This upsets his rhythm and in the long run will upset his disposition. When I start concentrated instruction on hands and arms, I stand beside the rider, whose horse is standing still, and, bracing my forearm on the horse's shoulder, I offer the rider one finger just above the withers, where the hands would normally hold the reins. (Fig. 76.) I then ask the rider to hold onto my finger and rise up and down as if posting to the trot. As the rider rises up and pulls on my finger, I immediately say, "Ouch!" The student invariably looks surprised, not having noticed that as he rose, he tried to take his hand up, too. Because he was holding onto me, he couldn't bring his hand up, so he balanced himself on my finger. He doesn't really hurt me, but that amount of pull would certainly be distracting and uncomfortable on the horse's mouth. So the rider tries again, being careful not to pull my finger.

As you try this experiment, you will notice that when you rise, you have to open your elbow joint quite wide to leave your hands quiet and still as you rise up. If you do not let the elbows open, your hands will go up with your body. The elbow joints must close equally as you sit down. This opening and closing of the elbows is comparable to the amount you must open and close your knees in the rising trot. Remember this new sensation. (Fig. 77.)

76. Rider holding instructor's finger. If she pulls the finger when she rises, as if in the trot, she has a stiff elbow.

77. The angles of the elbow and the knee open and close as we rise to the trot.

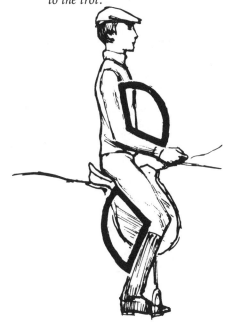

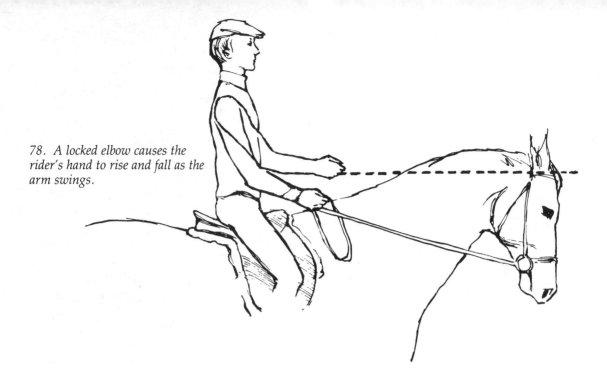

*78. A locked elbow causes the rider's hand to rise and fall as the arm swings.*

Any forward or backward motion you make with your hands will involve the elbow joints as well as the shoulder joints. One cannot work without the other. With no reins in your hands, try moving your arms back and forth as you might in following a horse's head at a walk. As you do this, try to point toward your horse's mouth. Most people, when they first try this exercise, will swing their upper arm all right, but will point to the horse's ears with the lower arm and hand. (Fig. 78:) It is quite a revelation to realize how much the elbow must open to allow the hand to point toward the horse's mouth.

Now walk on, allowing your hands and arms to follow the horse's head. Your forearm and rein should be in a straight line, whether seen from the side or from above. (Figs. 79a–d.) To maintain this line, your hands will have to be held higher when the horse carries his head high and lower when he carries it down. His head and neck swing a lot at a walk, and he must feel that you are constantly, delicately, with him, maintaining soft, even contact with his mouth. Your upper arm must hang freely from the shoulder like a stone on the end of a rope. The oiled joints of the shoulder and elbow must follow the fingers as they softly feel the horse's mouth.

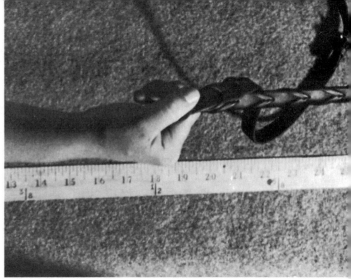

a. Correct straight line as seen from the side.

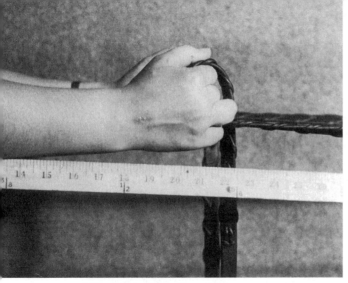

b. Correct straight line as seen from above.

79. The straight line from elbow to bit.

c. Incorrect: wrists broken outward, as seen from above.

d. Incorrect: wrists broken inward, as seen from above.

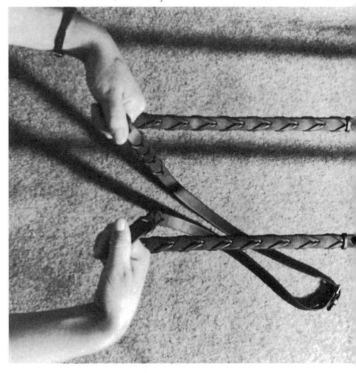

Once you have the shoulders and arms under control, stand still again and think about the wrists and fingers in relation to the forearm. Basically you must hold the rein with your thumb on top of it as it passes between the index finger and thumb. This keeps the rein from slipping. It passes out of your hand between your little finger and your ring finger.

Do not hold your hand flat, knuckles up, nor twisted with your thumb outward. The thumb knuckles should be up and angled very slightly toward each other. (Figs. 81a & b.)

There are two bones in your forearm. When you turn your hand so that the knuckles are horizontal, those two bones cross each other in a locked position. If, however, you turn your hand so that the knuckles are nearly vertical, you will find that the two bones run almost parallel, as viewed from above. (Figs. 82a & b.) This relationship between the two bones permits the hand to be more sensitive and responsive when the knuckles are held vertically. As for the tightness of the grip, imagine that you are holding a little bird in each hand with the head coming out between the index finger and thumb. (Fig. 80.) You must not squeeze the birds so hard that you might hurt them, or hold them so loosely that you'll lose them. You must also keep their heads up, so as not to bang them against each other. You can also pretend that you are holding a partially squeezed sponge in your hand. Hold it, but don't squeeze out all the water.

*80. Hold your reins as if they were little birds. Don't squeeze them or turn them so that their heads bang together.*

*81. Thumb side of the hand should be up.*

*a. Correct: thumbs up.*

*b. Incorrect: knuckles up.*

*a. Correct: thumb on top, bones of forearm parallel.*

*b. Incorrect: knuckles up, bones of forearm crossed and locked.*

*82. Hand and bones of forearm as seen from above.*

*83. Close the hands around the reins.*

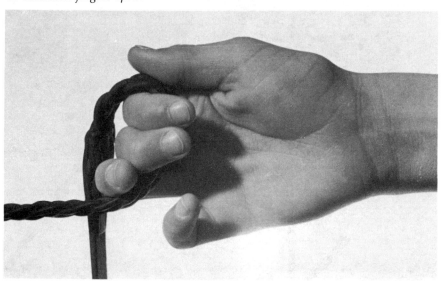

a. *Correct: fingertips touching palm.*

b. *Incorrect: fingers open.*

c. *Incorrect: fingers clenched too tightly.*

As you hold the reins, close your hands so that the knuckles are bent and *the tips of your fingers touch your palms.* Do not grab. (Figs. 83a–c.) If you ride with your reins near the tips of the fingers and the knuckles straight, you will not only deprive yourself of the use of some very useful joints—the knuckles—but the reins may also slip through your fingers.

Exercise your hands without the reins. Open them wide, spread the fingers apart, close them up, open and shut them repeatedly, bend your knuckles, wiggle your fingers. Try to realize how many joints you have and how few you usually use. Now pick up the reins again, closing your fingers around them. When you are going to say something to your horse through your hands, the ring finger should be the one that starts the motion. The other fingers come along afterward. (Figs. 84a & b.) All too easily, as you start to use your hands, the thumb and index finger come toward your body and your ring finger gets left behind, too weak to be effective. This tendency also puts your hand in an awkward position—and, as you know, any awkward position causes tension.

*84. The ring finger should be closed.*

*a. Contact correct.*

*b. Ineffective contact with ring finger too straight and all fingers open.*

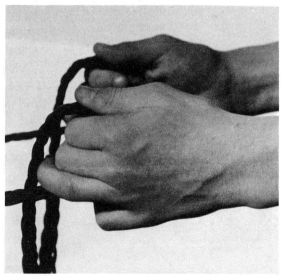

If just closing the ring finger with the other fingers following is not a sufficiently strong aid, then you can bend the hand down a little from the wrist with the knuckles still vertical; or you can slightly rotate the wrist, turning your closed fingers about 45 degrees outward. If even that is not enough, draw your elbows straight back.

Keep remembering that major motions come from the shoulder and elbow and only small ones come through the fingers. This does not mean that the fingers are less important. However, they are too often overused because you have not allowed the shoulder and elbow sufficient freedom.

Try imagining that your arms and reins from shoulder to bit are soft garden hoses, with water rushing through them and spurting way out ahead of the horse. (Fig. 85.) You will need to feel, and videotape internally, the sensation of that forward-rushing water—which is like the energy of the horse pouring through your arms, hands, and reins, beyond the bit. This will give the horse more confidence to move through your softer hands.

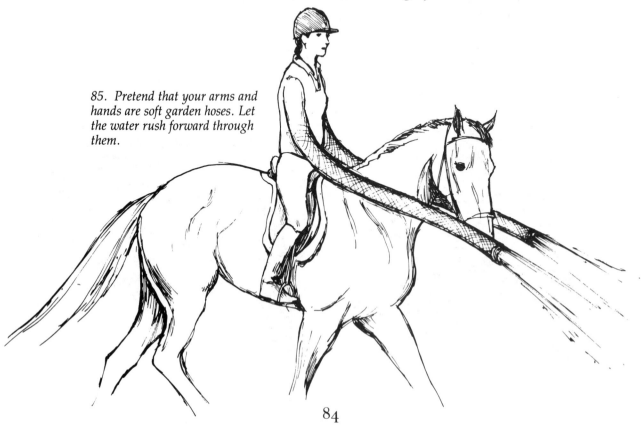

*85. Pretend that your arms and hands are soft garden hoses. Let the water rush forward through them.*

We cannot discuss hands without talking about *reward*. The primary reward for a horse in any correct movement is a momentary softening of the rider's hands. Most of the time, a good rider has contact with the horse's mouth. Let's call this normal contact. Depending upon the balance and sensitivity of the horse, it may be very light or fairly strong. Assume now that your horse is on the bit and you have a light, normal contact. You ask for a down transition, with your body and legs flowing into your hands. The reward should not come *after* the movement is finished, but rather be simultaneous with the end of the movement. In a down transition that includes several strides, you can give several of these rewards before the end of the transition. The softening is mostly in the hands. You must loosen the muscles of the palms and fingers without actually opening your fingers. This softening will also be partially reflected up through the wrists, elbows, and shoulders.

*What are the essentials of the correct use of hands?*
- Allow your elbow and shoulder joints to open and close freely.
- Hold your reins firmly, not too tightly or loosely.
- Use your fingers and wrists for small directions.
- Use your elbows and shoulders for major movements.
- Soften your hands at the end of specific movements as a reward to the horse.
- Carry little birds in hands.
- Use arms as soft garden hoses.

*What are the results of the correct use of hands?*
- A more direct feel of the horse's mouth.
- Steadier and softer hands.
- Your horse will go forward with consistent rhythm.

# 10

## Transitions

**A** consistently good down transition is one of the most important things you can learn in horsemanship. Visualize a free-galloping horse, without a rider, coming to a halt in no more than three or four strides. Watch his body during the down transition. He will round his back, dropping his head and neck. (Figs. 86a–d.) This allows him to bring the hind legs farther under his body with

*86. Down transitions, good and bad.*

*a. Cantering horse.*

*b. Horse stops lightly in balance.*

*c. Cantering horse.*

*d. Horse stops unbalanced and pounds down on his forelegs with a hollow, stiff back.*

each stride, which in turn permits his weight to shift back within his body. These movements allow him to have a balanced stop, with weight well distributed on his four feet. If, instead, he had hollowed his back and raised his head—a position we often see under saddle—he would have landed heavily on his forehand, front feet bracing and pounding into the ground, with very little weight on his hind feet. This latter scenario is a disaster, certainly to be avoided at all costs when riding.

The key to success lies in not jamming your seat bones onto the horse's back, but allowing him to round his back under your light, but following seat. With your horse still, sitting balanced and without stirrups, center yourself and grow up and down from your center. Recollect the spruce-tree image. (See Fig. 59.) Don't stretch, just allow your body to grow, always looking ahead with your eyes. (Fig. 87.) Notice again your increased body weight down the

*87. In a down transition, grow up as well as down to open your seat and receive your horse's rounding back.*

88. *Rider allowing knee to drop toward helper's finger.*

89. *Drop your stubby legs down the sides of your horse like a clothespin on a line.*

saddle through the front of your upper thighs, lightening your buttocks. You have not tightened your thighs, changed the level of your pelvis, or removed your buttocks or seat bones. You have only inwardly transferred some of your weight slightly forward in your body. By centering and growing, you opened and widened your seat. This allowed your horse to round his back and fill up your seat as he will need to do in a down transition.

As you discovered in the stubby-legs exercise (Chapter 7), the upper fronts of your thighs drop over the stirrup bars close to the sides of the pommel. With the help of gravity, this base provides firm support for the transition without muscular effort and will protect your crotch from the pommel.

Have a helper put a finger about one-eighth inch below the bottom of your knee. You will realize that growing will allow your knee to touch his finger. (Fig. 88.) As you drop your knees and the fronts of your thighs correctly, you will find that your shoulders stay balanced. The weight on your seat bones and buttocks lightens as it's transferred down the sides of the saddle in front of the stirrup leathers. This allows the horse to round his back beneath you. You will find yourself well forward, yet upright; the horse cannot tip the top of you forward once your thighs are heavily anchored and holding you. If you must take a more solid hold with your reins, you have a correct base from which to meet his pull. If your horse is light in your hands, you can give very precise aids because of the same solid base. Don't squeeze your legs against the saddle. The action of the upper legs around the horse is like that of the old-fashioned wooden clothespin on a line. It doesn't bring its sides together but does become increasingly firm as it drops down. (Fig. 89.)

As your knee drops when your foot is in the stirrup, the lower leg will be displaced slightly farther back on your horse's side. This is exactly where you want your lower leg to be during a down transition. Why? It's the same as what you would do instinctively if someone grabbed you around the middle: You'd want to double up. Similarly, if you place your legs a little farther back on the horse, he'll want to bring his hind legs under him. To move him forward, you must use repeated leg pressures and re-leases. He brings his hind legs under and pushes off from there. To slow down, you maintain a steady leg for sup-port—whatever amount is needed to keep the horse's hind legs under you and bring his balance back. Through-out, be sure not to press on the stirrups; leave your ankles soft and fluttery, with deep heels.

Your hands in the meantime will have closed enough to say "No" quietly and precisely to any impulse the horse may have had to go forward off your legs. The moment he obeys, you must immediately ease your hands back to normal pressure. The hind feet walk up into your hands; your hands do not move back toward your body and toward the horse's hind end. Any hand activity is a result of your aids to his body and quarters, not a cause. The sequence of aids for the down transition becomes 1) seat, 2) legs, 3) hands. During the transition, you will feel your hip joints opening toward your hands—never the hands coming to your hips. You'll increasingly feel that the control of your horse comes from your center, not above your diaphragm or below your stubby legs. You'll also be very conscious of the clothespin image mentioned above.

To put all this into practice, first try a lot of walk-halt transitions without stirrups. Remember the following: en-closing seat, elastic hip joints, and soft, long lower back. Center yourself and grow; walk the hind legs of the horse up into your hands. Breathe out during this transition. To prove the value of breathing out, try holding your breath during the next transition. You'll soon see that the horse obeys less readily.

Now breathe out again and walk your horse freely forward. Make the down transition to a halt; in doing so, try to receive every pulsation of the horse's back right up to the very last step. This will result in your horse stop-ping promptly and completely instead of winding down slowly.

Once you achieve the halt, leave your legs quietly enclosing your horse's sides. You will still be communicat-ing with him, still thinking forward even though you are stationary.

When you first use your stirrups for the down transi-

*a. Horse balanced and forward in the trot.*

*b. Rider stiff and bracing, causing horse to lose forward energy. Note resistance in horse.*

*90. Bad down transition.*

*c. Horse goes into a stiff walk.*

tion, you want to avoid pushing down or forward on them. (Figs. 90a–c.) This is the tendency for almost anyone first learning deep-seat down transitions. Pushing on the stirrups results in the stiffening and tensing of the ankles, knees, hips, and body. When you dropped your thighs and knees down without stirrups, there was no problem; but stirrups get in the way and block the knees from dropping. (Figs. 91a–c.) To avoid this, think about how you kneel. To kneel you must get your feet back out of the way and open your hip joints forward to allow the knees to drop. As your knees drop down unhindered, your soft ankles enable the insides of your lower legs to have contact with your horse just below the saddle, six to eight inches behind the girth. This position tells your horse to bring his hind legs under him as his back fills your open seat. You will have the full benefit of your

a. Horse balanced and forward in the trot.

b. Horse forward and round in transition.

91. Good aown transition.

c. Horse comes into a balanced, forward walk.

sensitive, powerful seat controlling your horse's hind legs.

When you can do good walk-halt transitions, you can do down transitions at any gait. Don't jam your horse into the transition. Allow him the strides he needs for balance. As you continue to practice, you'll be able to reduce the strides to a minimum, but throughout keep the feeling of a dance through the transition, with his hind legs stepping under to carry his body lightly.

Up transitions can be beautiful. The horse simply flows from one gait to another in perfect unison with the rider. To do this, both horse and rider must be attentive and aware of each other, with the rider alerting the horse first by centering himself. He can feel the receptiveness of the horse and can time his motions so that horse and rider advance together.

*a. Horse already feeling tension in the rider before transition.*

*b. During transition to trot, rider stiffens, her center is left behind, and the horse is unhappy.*

*92. Bad up transition.*

*c. Horse then moves into stiff-legged trot with a hollow back.*

Unfortunately, awkward and even disastrous up transitions are all too common. You may clearly say to the horse, "Move forward," but then fail to go forward yourself. When your center gets left behind, you fall down heavily on the horse's back. The horse says "Ouch" by hollowing his back and leaving his hind legs out behind him. At the same time, the loss of balance causes the rider to catch the horse's mouth with the bit, making him stiffen his neck in front of the withers and raise his head. The horse will soon acquire this bad habit of automatically raising his head and hollowing his back for a stride or two on every up transition. (Figs. 92a–c.)

In order to avoid such awkward moments, start by playing your inner videotape of a lovely transition. (Figs. 93a–c.) Remember that during the up transition, the horse's activity starts with the powerful hind legs and their big bending joints—stifles, hocks, and fetlocks. The initial thrust must come from your center. (Fig. 94.) Feel

a. Horse and rider relaxed and soft before the transition.

b. During transition to trot, horse rounds up beneath rider. Rider's center stays forward with the horse's motion.

93. Good up transition.

c. Horse trots off soft and round, with energy coming from behind, up through the withers and neck.

your following seat increase its motion, and keep the motion coming in rhythm with the horse. Remember to use your Four Basics. You must be with your horse's forward movement from the very first part of the first footfall. If you miss the first stride, it is already too late to catch up.

As you build energy in your center, keep your legs near the girth, where the horse's nervous system reacts best to directions for forward motion. Use small squeezes as needed. The horse gets the message from both your seat and your legs.

Think forward and up from your center. Feel your horse's rhythm. With this lively action of your seat, you ask the horse to fill up underneath you, to round his back, and to move out. Your hands must soften to release his front end. He should flow forward from behind, his energy coming up and out through the withers and down again to the bit.

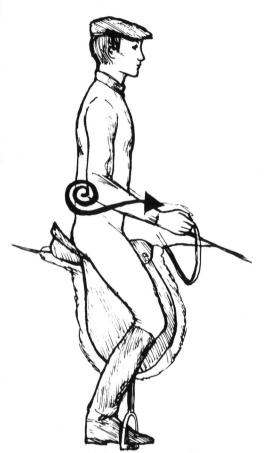

94. *Churn up the energy in your center and send it forward.*

When you have all these elements set up properly, even a lethargic horse will surprise you in the up transition. I am not saying that you will never use your whip or spurs. Horses, just like people, are individual beings. Fortunately for us, they usually like to please us. However, they can also be willful, playful, stubborn, or just plain naughty. At these times discipline must be used—preferably with the whip. It should be quick, positive, and as forceful as needed (which sometimes may have to be quite forceful), but never brutal. A positive response from the horse must receive an immediate end to the discipline and the resumption of your asking aids. The horse should now be more ready to listen to them. If you must use the whip to make your horse listen to forward aids, make sure you do not pull on his mouth or bang his back when he jumps forward, out from under you, in obedience. Throw your reins loose and let your shoulders swing back if you must, but do not hurt your horse as he attempts to respond. Then take time to reassemble yourself and start to ride him correctly again. You will find him more responsive.

Practice many halt-walk transitions, interspersed with some trotting to freshen your horse's interest. You will know that you have learned to do a correct up transition when you feel the horse lengthening and widening his back under you as he moves. You'll feel him raise his neck slightly just in front of the withers as he reaches out and a little down with his neck at the poll. When you can do this well from the halt to the walk, begin doing walk-trot and then walk-trot-canter transitions. With practice, using your Four Basics and correct use of aids, your balance will improve, your horse will become more happily responsive, and your transitions will become things of beauty.

*What are the essentials of correct transitions?*

- Use your Four Basics prior to and during the transition.
- Breathe out during the transition.
- Keep the energy flowing from behind.

*For a down transition:*

- Center and grow up and down.
- Lighten your feet with your soft lower leg back and against the horse.
- Allow the clothespin to drop, not pinch.
- Feel the horse fill your open seat.
- Close the hands enough to prevent forward movement.
- Reward the horse with softened hands and seat.
- Think forward even in the down transition.

*For an up transition:*

- Feel your and the horse's energy lift forward and up from behind through your center.
- Center and grow.
- Flow forward with your horse from the first instant.
- Soften your hands to release the front end.

*What are the results of a correct transition?*

- Forward energy is maintained.
- Horse will round his back and not resist the transition.
- Horse remains light on his feet.
- Horse becomes more attentive and responsive.
- Communication with your horse improves.

# 11

## Sitting Trot

It is commonly felt that the best way to learn to sit to the trot is by attrition, to do it again and again until you get shaken into it. People spend many hours having someone lunge them on a horse, while both rider and horse suffer miserably from the bouncing and jarring movements. This situation can be improved by first absorbing a few techniques. You can learn to sit to the trot in a comparatively short time, making it less traumatic for both you and the horse.

You have spent a lot of time at the walk, working on the close, three-point seat following the motion of the horse. You then began to allow the torso to grow up while the thighs grow down for down transitions. Both of these techniques are necessary in the sitting trot.

The trot is a two-beat gait. At each beat, the horse's diagonal feet touch the ground. At that point, the horse's body is as low as it can go. In between beats, the horse's body rises into suspension. Then it drops again. If the bottom of your seat is to stay in contact with the horse's back, it must follow all of that motion. While practicing down transitions you allowed your body and stubby legs to grow down. (Fig. 95.) In growing down, the front of your hips opened, but your pelvis remained level. In the sitting trot, you allow this to happen with every stride. I like to think of a sitting trot as a one-one rhythm, compared to the one-two rhythm of the rising trot. So, on every "one" beat of a sitting trot, you should allow yourself to fall downhill with the horse. In between, you allow the horse to fill your seat and bring you back up to normal.

Imagine a skier on a slope full of moguls. While his head and shoulders remain level, his skis and legs drop down between each mogul and rise softly up again on top of the next mogul. (Fig. 96.) Or try picturing the wheels of a car moving up and down over a bumpy road; the wheels bounce up and down while the body of the car moves along smoothly above them.

95. In the sitting trot, let your stubby legs grow down over the stirrup bars.

96. In the sitting trot, let your feet and legs bounce down and up, as if you were skiing moguls.

On a horse, you cannot make yourself follow the motion. You must allow the horse to do it for you, just as you did at the walk. To keep the hips soft, you must also keep the head and neck free and balanced and the back long and wide. Your lower back should not collapse and hollow—that would roll your pelvis on the horse's back. Don't let your back become stiff, either. It would be nice if the back could actually lengthen and shorten, but you will have to settle for imagining it as a strong rubber column, one that has some freedom of motion, one that can act somewhat as a cushion but cannot collapse.

There is also a slight cushioning effect in the pelvic region. You will remember from Chapter 5 that the spine is fused into the back of the pelvis at the sacrum. As a result, any weight carried by the spine will pass downward through the back of the pelvis. The legs, on the other hand, connect with the pelvis near the middle at the hip joints. The seat bones are directly under these joints. Thus any upward thrust from the legs will go up through the front of the pelvis, which becomes a sort of bridge or cantilever between the upward and downward forces, allowing for some spring or cushioning between them and avoiding possible jarring.

The cushioning in the pelvis will happen only if the pelvis is level. If you hollow the lower back and tip the front of the pelvis down, the sacrum will be directly above the seat bones, and all possibility of a cushion is lost—producing discomfort for you and the horse. The buttocks, which are below the sacrum, also absorb the motion. They act as a cushion and you can think of them as nice firm pads of foam rubber.

After centering yourself and breathing down through your center, try trotting for three or four strides and then do a smooth down transition to a walk. Again, breathe out during the down transition. Do this several times. At the trot you need to have a really soft and quiet lower back, and with the small number of strides, you won't stiffen. The down transition accentuates the down stretch, which helps you find the feel of the motion.

Try the exercise we used earlier at the walk, stretching your arm straight up over your head. (See Fig. 62.) Let all your body hang down and away from your arm, with your front feeling elastic and stretchable. This exercise will help to separate and free your lower body. Temporarily allow your lower back too much motion; let the horse wobble your pelvis back and forth completely, until you realize how much motion you have to deal with.

As you trot, change hands over your head occasionally. Now go to your center and become aware of the feeling that your pelvis is becoming heavier, especially in the back. Allow it to become quiet in the saddle and remain level and balanced on the middle of the seat bones. As the pelvis becomes steady, it will in turn quiet the lower back. Now think of the rubber-column image—the back having free motion, but not collapsing. Your opening and closing the hip joints will by now be absorbing most of the motion of the horse.

Imagine, once again, that you are the puppet hung by a string from the top of your head. (Fig. 97.) The string suspends your head from the sky, while all the rest of you hangs down from your head and neck. Then imagine that you, this puppet, have a lot of wet sand stuck up in your neck, shoulders, and rib cage. Gradually, this sand dries out and starts to run downhill like dry sand in the summer sun. It keeps trickling down, streaming into and through your pelvis, legs, and feet. As it runs down, the lower part of your body gets heavier and heavier. The upper parts become emptier and lighter as the sand streams away, until you are left with an empty shell for an upper body, with your neck and head still suspended from the string. Now visualize this sand running down all over your horse's back and then feel the back rise up through the sand to fill your seat.

97. *Imagine that you are a puppet hung from above by a string attached to the top of your head.*

Try another exercise: Starting at a walk, without your stirrups and with your seat deep and level, draw your heels up toward your buttocks. Keep them up there and spread your arms out sideways. (Fig. 98.) If you have no one to lead your horse, spread your arms as far as the reins will let you. As you walk, realize how free and independent your lower body can be if you remove some of the tension of the lower legs. Now, in the normal riding position, try to take this freedom of motion of the hip joints, buttocks, and lower back into the sitting trot. Let your legs surround the horse normally, using gravity, not grip.

*98. At the walk, draw your heels up toward your buttocks, spread your arms out, and really open your front and hip joints.*

*99. Sitting trot.*

*a. Good sitting trot. Rider's seat deep and soft, horse moving forward happily.*

*b. Poor sitting trot. Rider's braced leg and rigid posture cause tension in horse and result in stiff-legged trot.*

When you feel comfortable with very short periods of the sitting trot, go for longer stretches before your down transition. If you begin to stiffen and bounce, return to the walk and start again. Do this until you are so confident in your sitting that you can always find that deep, soft position by centering yourself with soft eyes. (Figs. 99a & b.) Keep the sitting trot slow at first; the faster the horse trots, the more difficult it will be for you to stay with the motion.

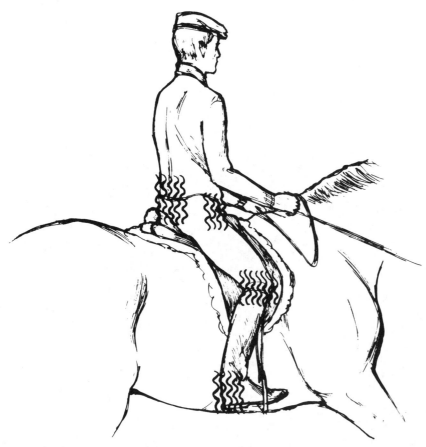

*100. If you stiffen any of the spots indicated, your neck, head, shoulders, and hands will bounce.*

There is a lot of motion from a horse's body to be absorbed by yours. Perhaps 90 percent of this motion can be taken up by the free use of your hip joints, knees, and ankles. Think again of the image of a car's wheels absorbing bumps over a rough road. If the hip joints, knees, and ankles are stiff, the horse's motion goes up your body and produces a kind of whiplash effect at the top, making the head bob and the shoulders jump. The motion of the horse obviously has not been absorbed. When you see a rider's head wobbling, it's almost always because he has stiff hip joints. Since good hands are dependent upon a quiet upper body, a good seat is absolutely essential. This seat, together with soft hip joints and fluttery knees and ankles, free to open and close with the horse's every move, are the key to the sitting trot. (Fig 100.) In addition, if you are able to receive the upward pulsations of the horse's back through your body, your horse will respond with brilliant movement.

I remember watching Harry Boldt at the 1976 Olympics in Montreal. His shoulders were still, wide, square, and balanced over his pelvis, and his hands were soft and quiet. His tailcoat concealed his lower back, but his hip joints were visibly free. There was total unity with his horse. Two experienced men behind me were talking, and one remarked, "You may hear people saying how stiff the German riding is, but that man's lower body can't be stiff. If it were, his shoulders couldn't be so quiet."

I later watched Walter Christenson, also from Germany, at clinics he gave in the town of Harvard, Massachusetts. He rode either in a short jacket or sweater, so that I was able to see his lower back and hips. With soft knees and ankles, and with a quiet, supple back, his hip joints were moving sufficiently to absorb all the motion of the horse without any exaggeration of movement. I never saw the muscles of his buttocks or the bottoms of his thighs tighten. He rode with beautifully balanced suppleness.

### *What are the essentials of the correct sitting trot?*

- Keep growing up and down from your center.
- Follow the horse's forward and downward motion with your quiet lower back, opening hip joints, and following thighs.
- Allow the hip joints to open and close.
- Allow fluttery knees and ankles.
- Receive the upward pulsations of the horse's back.
- Keep your buttocks and backs of your legs wide and soft.
- Keep breathing to keep your back supple, not rigid.
- Use gravity, not grip.

### *What are the results of the correct sitting trot?*

- Unity with your horse.
- Increased communication with your horse.
- Improved balance, softness, and sense of rhythm.
- Improvement of the horse's movement.

# 12

## Circles and Turns

**R**iding a horse in a circle may seem like a simple maneuver. In a circle, the bend of the horse's body from poll to tail should be the same as the arc of the circle. For instance, a circle six meters in diameter will require more bend in the horse than a circle twenty meters in diameter. But when you look closer, you can see many awkward variations of resistance and lack of rapport between horse and rider. You often see the horse bending the wrong way around the circle or turn, or bent only at his shoulder, popping the shoulder out. (Figs. 101a & b.) Sometimes you see a horse not bent at all, with the hind legs tracking a bigger circle than the front. And sometimes a horse is bent too much or not at all, yet tracking the hind feet inside the front feet. These contortions (and others) are the result of stiffness in the body and joints of the horse, or resistance to the rider, or a combination of both.

Imagine that the horse's body, poll to tail, is a bow. To bend a bow, you not only push out the middle, but both ends must be secured. The active inside leg, which bends the bow and creates impulsion, should be used at the girth in harmony with the horse's rhythm. Any stiffness will cause resistance from the horse. He does not want to bend his body around an iron bar, but will happily curl around a soft, sensitive leg—the one you get from leg-lengthening. (See Fig. 56.)

The outside leg secures one end of the bow by preventing the horse's quarters from swinging out; it must therefore be placed farther back on the horse's side. This outside leg must be firm, constant, and quiet unless impulsion has been so badly lost that both legs are momentarily needed to restore it. (See Fig. 55.)

The outside rein secures the other end of the bow by keeping the shoulder from popping out and controlling the degree of bend. In addition, it maintains the pace and should remain taut and constant. In order to put pressure

*101. Incorrect circles.*

*a. Stiff horse bent the wrong way.*

*b. Horse popping his shoulder.*

on the neck, the outside hand can come above the crest of the horse's neck, but never across it. Directing the outside hand toward the pommel has a stabilizing effect on the horse. This rein must not float at all, but must never be harsh.

The inside rein has a more varied role. It can lead the horse into the turn lightly, but you must not hang on it or the horse will resist and stiffen. In a circle, you should just see the arch of the horse's inside eye and nostril. The inside hand can aid the inside leg in securing the bend. As the edge of the eye comes into view and the horse softens his body on that side, your hand must simultaneously ease; thus, when the horse is moving correctly and softly, the inside hand has only the slightest contact. It is not a supporting rein, like the outside one, but an asking and giving rein.

In circles and turns, the use of the seat, legs, and hands must eventually become synchronized to produce this bent-bow effect, but you must first learn how to apply the aids separately, using your body correctly.

Remember the feeling of stubby legs? Now drop your outside leg back from your hip joint. (Notice this takes your thigh back about an inch, and your lower leg back three to six inches.) Then, when you sink the heel back, you will have a feeling of length from your shoulder to your heel. With your horse at a halt, imagine you are executing a right circle. Now drop your inside stubby leg down in front of your stirrup leather. This motion will lower your knee and tend to push your lower leg down and under the horse near the girth, provided you allow your knee and ankle to remain supple.

First at a walk, then at a trot, go out and ride lots of large circles, figure eights, and serpentines on a rather loose rein, without stirrups, mentally using only your stubby legs. It is interesting to see how clearly a horse understands the aid of *only* stubby legs for turns, circles, and even down transitions. Try it, making sure you really reposition your stubby legs for each change of direction. The inside one reaches down rhythmically, becoming an active leg, while the outside stubby leg lies positively and quietly farther behind the girth. With the top of that leg rolled forward and the rest of it stretched back, you will clearly feel what is meant by "the flat of the thigh against the horse." Even the inside stubby leg will feel flat on the horse.

It's a lovely feeling to become more aware of the sides of the horse. One student said she had always thought of the saddle simply as something to sit on, but now she realized that her searching, stubby legs found the sides of the saddle to be very important.

When you put your stirrups on and add your lower legs to the stubby legs, imagine that you have no knees, only pieces of string that attach your shin to your thigh. Because of the string, the lower leg will not appreciably affect your thigh position, while the thigh *will* affect your lower leg position. Stretch your outside leg back from the hip with your thigh flat, knee soft, lower leg against the horse, foot parallel to the horse's side, or as close to as possible, and your ankle soft and flexed. You should feel that your heel sinks through the stirrup, back and downward, not with pressure, but in a relaxed way that ultimately allows the outside seat bone and buttock to settle comfortably on your horse's back.

This positioning and use of your legs, with the dropping of the inside stubby leg, combines with the inside sliding seat bone and helps urge the horse forward on the circle with very little effort on your part. Often, when you actively use the inside seat bone and leg, the outside seat bone is accidentally raised and the inside of your body collapses in the direction of the turn. Also, the entire pelvis will often slip to the outside. These errors will not occur if the stubby legs are used correctly.

Now that you have control over your legs and seat during your circles and turns, think about your upper body. This next step in improving circles starts again at the halt. The whole body is involved to some degree in any motion, on or off a horse. A good place to become aware of this is in circles. When you are walking on the ground and start to turn either to the right or to the left, you will automatically swivel your shoulders very slightly in the direction of the turn. Note that both shoulders change position—when one goes forward, the other comes back. It is a small motion; it squares the shoulders in the direction you want to go.

On a horse you add another dimension. To turn right, you move your right shoulder back a little and place your left leg back on your horse's side. You have now turned your entire body into a swivel from the soles of your feet right through to the top of your head. Your pelvis, which is in the middle, is the least involved. The gear that *creates* the entire motion, however, is in your center, and the upper and lower movement all stems from there.

Let's get the top half in motion first. Put your arms out sideways, horizontally. Think of a ship's mast going up through your body, with your shoulders and arms as the yardarm. You can swivel around the well-greased mast all you want, but since you can't bend it, you will have no trouble in keeping the yardarm from tilting off the horizontal. Try swiveling your upper body with shoulders, arms, and head as one piece, keeping your pelvis quiet. Note how easy it is to hold your shoulders level when your arms are horizontal. (Fig. 103a.) Notice the openness of your upper body. Keep swiveling, and when you feel that you are swinging freely, gradually lower your arms, bringing them forward into a circular position as if holding a large beach ball—your hands should be about six inches above the withers, palms slightly up, shoulders hanging very wide. (Fig. 103b.) Continue the swivel motion back and forth in this new position and notice from your center the circular sensation within your body around the mast. It should feel balanced, soft, and open. Now, still rotating, quietly drop your elbows to your sides, leaving your hands where they were, still moving with your shoulders. Gradually reduce the degree of swivel to a small motion and you will find it to be a quite refined, delicate movement of the upper body—perfect for riding a circle on your horse. (Fig. 103c.) If you now break the rules and look down at your hands, you will also find that because your arms and hands move with your shoulders, they are displaced sideways just enough to lay the outside rein on the horse's neck exactly as needed, without any other action than that created by your center.

Now try swiveling with your legs only. As we did earlier, first place one stubby leg back, and drop the other straight down. Then reverse your stubby leg position as you swivel the other way. You will have to organize the balance of the upper body; and to do this, you'll need to be very soft-eyed, using breathing and centering. Otherwise you will find your pelvis twisting and one buttock coming off the saddle as you alternately move each leg back. Don't try for large swings. Keep them small and correct.

Now try to coordinate the upper and lower movements. Start again with the arms out horizontally, then bring them down through the circle to lowered elbows and normal hands. Think it through carefully before you begin, because when the right shoulder goes back the left leg must go back, and vice versa. Keep your mast vertical, without any sideways contortions. Keep your lower back long and both buttocks evenly on the saddle. (Fig. 103d.) I like to walk behind my students during this exercise to make sure both buttocks stay soft in the saddle. Remember that your head turns no more than your shoulders, and that you're using a well-oiled gear—your center.

You have seen those red-and-white-striped barbershop poles that turn continuously, giving the impression they are forever flowing gently upward with their motion. (Fig. 102.) Now, when you try turning your horse in circles and

*102. Be a barbershop pole. Spin clockwise to go right and counter-clockwise to go left.*

103a. Swiveling with arms horizontal; pelvis remains quiet.

b. Swiveling while holding imaginary beach ball.

c. Swiveling with elbows dropped; hands move with shoulders, resulting in correct position for a turn.

d. Legs and shoulders swiveling in opposite directions, in correct position for a left turn.

104. *While learning to open the inside shoulder on a turn, try dropping the inside arm behind your thigh.*

serpentines, imagine that from the soles of your feet right out through the top of your head you are a barbershop pole. When you turn right, the pole spins clockwise; when you turn left, it spins counterclockwise. One student who rides all dressage levels through Grand Prix said, after practicing this exercise, "Now I know that when my instructor tells me to position myself before a change, I must take time to change the direction of the barbershop pole."

Using all of yourself in this manner, ride some twenty-meter circles and serpentines at the walk with a light contact; then at both a rising and a sitting trot. You will probably find it takes less effort than you have used previously. The horse will respond willingly because your comprehensive aids are very clear to him and not at all bothersome.

For those who have problems with the barbershop pole concept, there are some other images that may help. If you're having difficulty truly opening the inside shoulder, try taking both reins in the outside hand and then drop your inside arm straight down so that the hand hangs behind your thigh when you rotate your shoulders. (Fig. 104.) This creates an open sensation in the front of your body; it is exactly what you should feel when you have *both* hands on the reins.

When you swivel correctly, your hands will move slightly sideways. Look down and watch this happen. Then swivel again and force your hands to remain stationary over the horse's withers. Notice how hard it is to swivel the body. Many people fail to allow the hands to move with the shoulders and thereby block the flow of the turn. They often turn their head and neck under the illusion that the upper body has also turned. But it hasn't.

So pretend you have eyes on your chest. (Fig. 105.) In order to look around the bend, you must turn your upper body so your chest faces the intended direction. You must get the inside shoulder out of the way so the eyes in your chest have a clear view. As you do this, your nose should be directly over your sternum; this will keep your head steady. In jumping you may need to turn your head more, but in flat work remember that with soft eyes you can see more than half the arena at one time, so there is no need to turn your head if your body is involved. A turned head can put your delicate body balance off-center. If the eyes in your chest can see clearly around the bend, you have moved your head and shoulders correctly.

After you have been doing these swiveling exercises at the walk and trot and you find yourself dropping the inside shoulder as you turn, remember the yardarm on the mast that can swing only horizontally. Dropping the shoulder particularly causes problems when you are riding forward, because it collapses the inside of the rib cage and lumbar spine, throwing weight onto the outside seat bone and pushing the pelvis off-center to the outside. So, as you turn the yardarm, try breathing into your inside lower ribs so that they don't collapse but instead keep you erect and poised. Your body axis should never tip to the side more than your horse's axis. Any tip is very slight in most balanced flatwork, due to the slow speed of most movements.

If your teacher asks you to move your inside hip forward in a turn, be aware that you have already accomplished this by dropping your stubby leg. Trying to force your hip forward more will be difficult and disastrous!

Still another way to ride turns more effectively is to *feel* that you are moving the horse with energy generated *from*

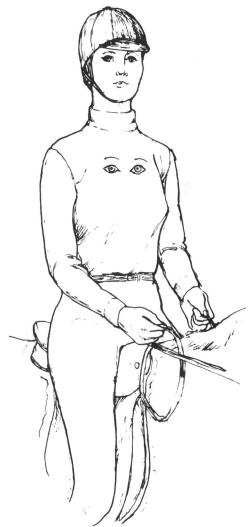

105. *To help your upper body swivel, imagine you have eyes in your chest that look in the direction of the turn.*

*that side of your center toward which you are turning.* In other words, breathe and center in the right side to turn right, and vice versa.

By the time you know how to place your stubby legs and swivel your shoulders correctly, learning circles and turns, it becomes very easy to control the horse's hindquarters and forehand, bending him in the arc of the desired turn. It is an invaluable package of aids that directs and contaihs the whole of your horse through the turn. From your center, using very little muscle and with a minimum of motion and effort, you have correctly synchronized and placed your pelvis, legs, torso, head, shoulders, and hands for turning.

I would now like to discuss the extra energy needed to perform circles and turns. Because it takes more effort to turn than it does to follow a straight line, both horse and rider tend to lose energy (impulsion) during a circle or turn. An image of water rushing through a funnel helps riders really understand and feel the required forward energy coming from behind. Your legs, seat, arms, hands, and reins are the funnel. Your horse is the water. Hold both your arms out toward your horse's mouth and imagine the water rushing through you and out between your funnel arms.

The shape of the funnel directs the water, which comes from behind with a force great enough to drive it straight out. Both your arms, the side of the funnel, are receiving equal force from the water. If you now turn both arms somewhat to the right, which side of the funnel needs to be stronger to contain the force of the water? Since water under pressure prefers to travel in a straight line, the answer is the left arm, which, in a turn to the right, provides the greater resistance to the water. It is the outside wall of the funnel. This image will help you understand why, when riding a circle, the outside rein and leg must provide constant and sometimes strong contact—strong enough to resist the water's assault on it. (Fig. 106.)

106. *In a turn, imagine that the forward energy of the horse is water rushing through a curved funnel. The horse presses against the outside aids, just as water presses against the outer wall of the funnel.*

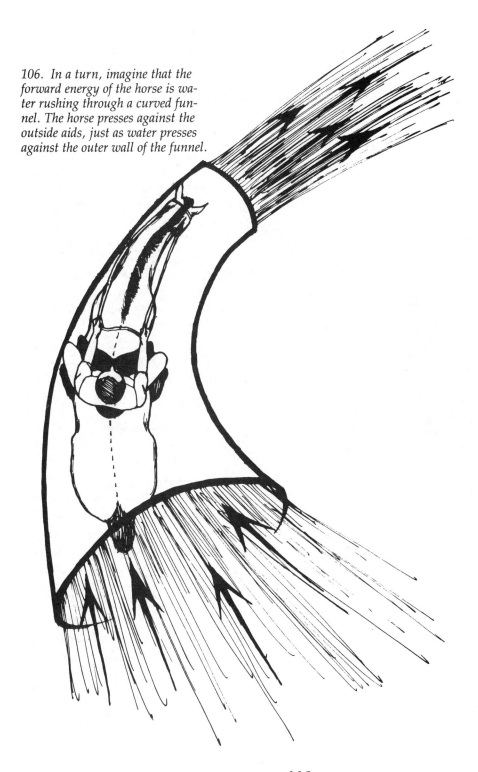

It is logical that the inside wall of the funnel, your left arm, need not be as strong. If you totally remove it, the water will just spill, disperse, and go nowhere. If you use it too hard to pull the horse around, it will squeeze and block the flow, retarding or even stopping the forward motion. Some inside rein is needed to shape the water and keep it flowing forward, but your grip must be light and playful.

What happens if someone turns off the water pressure behind you? The water stops running, of course. This means that even with the funnel all set correctly in the right direction, you won't get around the turn. The energy from behind is gone. Where does that water-pressure energy originate? It comes from your horse's hindquarters and is made active by your inside leg. If you keep this leg soft from your neck and shoulder all the way down, it can be very active and the horse will obey. A rigid and unforgiving leg tends to make the horse bend against it— bend the wrong way.

Now you understand the aids for circling and turning. To sum up, your outside leg and rein contain the horse's energy to make the turn; the inside rein keeps the funnel shape but in no way impedes that energy, and your inside leg keeps it streaming powerfully way out ahead of you. Even experienced riders have told me that this image, for the first time, made clear to them the reasons for the outside aids.

*107. Outside of the circle. Note the bend of the horse and balance of both horse and rider, and position of rider's leg.*

Using the combined images of the turning barbershop pole plus the water funnel, practice riding serpentines at a walk and trot. (Figs. 107 & 108.) As you start to cross the ring in each loop of the serpentine, play the next turn on your videotape. Position yourself and your horse for the turn and then ride through it. Remember to be soft in your neck and armpit and mold your horse with your soft inside seat bone, buttock, and lower leg while containing him with your outer leg and rein. Think of his inside hind foot coming forward to support the weight of his body with every stride. Hear and feel his rhythm and build mental energy from the center of your body to encourage the horse to go forward. Keep your chest eyes looking around the bend and feel the upward push of the strides through your horse's back.

*What are the essentials of riding circles and turns?*

- Use your Four Basics.
- Use your stubby legs down the front of the saddle, leaving your pelvis level.
- Place the outside leg back from the hip joint.
- Sink the outside leg down and back, foot parallel to the horse.
- Use the soft inside leg, both the top of the stubby leg and the lower leg, as well as the sliding seat bone, to bend and stimulate the horse.
- Rotate your shoulders and upper body slightly to let your chest eyes see around the bend.
- Keep your outside rein steady and supportive.
- Ask and give with your inside rein.
- Keep the water rushing through the funnel.
- Be a barbershop pole from the soles of your feet through the top of your head.

*108. Inside of the circle. Note the bend in the horse's body and the position of the rider's leg and torso.*

*What are the results of riding circles and turns?*

- Both seat bones remain on the horse, with the inside one free to slide.
- The rider's body is stable, balanced, and free.
- The horse maintains a correct bend on the circle.
- The horse moves forward with ease and in balance.

# 13

# Half Halts and Self-Carriage

## *Half Halts*

**W**hen my students have a good feel for riding, the Four Basics are solidly implanted in their technique. They have control and balance of the upper body, neck, and head. They ride with a long, wide back and resulting free hip joints. They are doing good circles and turns, with constant centering and growing. They can also do good down transitions. At this point I ask a series of questions.

The first question is "What effect does *centering* have on your body?" The answers vary: "It relaxes me . . . it makes me softer." "I am more comfortable." "I sit deeper . . . my center of gravity drops . . . my legs come under me." "I can feel what I am doing, and can also feel my horse better." All these are true. Then, finally, "It *balances* me." That is the word I am waiting for. Centering balances or rebalances your body, producing all the other results.

My next question is "Does your horse react to your centering, and if so, how?" Everyone is sure that the horse feels the centering. As to what he does in response, again, there are many answers: "He becomes softer . . . he moves with more fluid strides." "He is more responsive." "He moves forward better . . . he brings his hind legs under him." All these answers are true, too. Then suddenly someone realizes, "He rebalances himself!" Yes, that's it. When he feels you come into balance, he likes it and he fills up your seat by rounding and widening his back as he brings his hind legs under, lightens his forehand, and thus rebalances himself.

Then I ask my third question, "What is a half halt and why do you do it?" This almost always produces consternation and scowling faces. The other two questions brought dreamy smiles. Then come the answers, all correct as far as they go: "You do a half halt before you do something." "It is a preparation for your horse to change gait, or pace." "You drive the horse with your legs into your hands to make him bring his hind legs under." This last answer is often accompanied by the front of the rider's body and shoulders tightening and pulling together, hips and legs tensing—and an extra scowl.

So, I ask "What does this half halt basically do for your horse?" Then comes the revelation. "It rebalances him!" Yes, exactly. (Fig. 109.) If you think about it, you will realize that each time you centered yourself you were actually making a small half halt. How beautiful and simple it now is to comprehend. Half halts need no longer require scowling faces and tense bodies.

*109. Half halt for down transition, canter to trot. The horse rounds up under the rider as she rebalances. The rider's leg could be farther back.*

"Half halt" is a most unfortunate and misleading term. It has little to do with halting. Rebalance is a better word. However, since the term half halt is universally accepted, I am going to use it in the following pages.

A half halt almost always means greater engagement of the hind legs, bringing them farther under the horse's body so that the center of gravity comes back and the forehand can be lighter. A half halt is also full of inward forward motion, even though it does not necessarily increase or decrease speed. Before you ask your horse to make a different move, as from walk to trot, you must prepare him with a half halt, asking him to be attentive and rebalance his body so that he can dance into the next movement easily and with brilliance. You must also use the half halt to rebalance the horse as needed, throughout the movement. Be sure your hands lighten at the end of the half halt to reward your horse and allow him to go forward.

Up to this point in your training, everytime you have centered yourself you have performed a "mini" half halt, rebalancing the horse as well as yourself. You can make the half halt more powerful by simply adding to your centering any of the following: stronger legs into hands; legs into stronger hands; or inside leg into outside hand at a corner. You can whisper a half halt by simply centering yourself, but whether it is a whisper or a shout, it should never be a jam-the-rear-into-the-front process. It's more of a dance instead.

Lockie Richards, in his book *Dressage: Begin the Right Way,* has a beautiful section on the half halt that I recommend to any rider. He says, "All the rider needs to do is to correct his position, or carry himself more elegantly for a moment, by sitting tall and relaxing his seat, thus allowing the horse to come up to his seat bones and fill out between his legs. When the horse feels the rider carrying himself, he will usually respond immediately by picking himself up a little."

When riding a spirited horse who is pulling hard, you need to first slow him down and then maintain the pace. Think of doing it either in a series of half halts or small down transitions. Use your aides to ask, receive, and give in order to bring him down one degree. Repeat the aids several times to bring him down farther, and then use them as necessary to maintain your desired speed. After the repeated sequences, you have really slowed your horse. Thus you can see that it is possible to intermingle these three tools of centering, half halts, and down transitions for many purposes.

All these aids can be used in a multitude of degrees and combinations, so keep them ready in the pool of your right brain. I like to tell my students, "There is no way you can be too tall, or too deep, or too wide, or center yourself too often—or do too many half halts.

Now, when you work with your horse, you need only think "rebalance," whether you are centering or doing a half halt or down transition. This adds a new dimension to your riding and starts you on the road to *self-carriage* for your horse.

## *Self-Carriage for Horse and Rider*

What is self-carriage? It is a concept of the relationship between the hoofs of the horse and his body mass. Imagine the horse's body as a parallelogram, with four hoofed legs. The placement of the hoofs on the ground determines the stability of the body mass in relation to the oblong body mass.

*110. Relationship between horse's hoofs and body mass.*

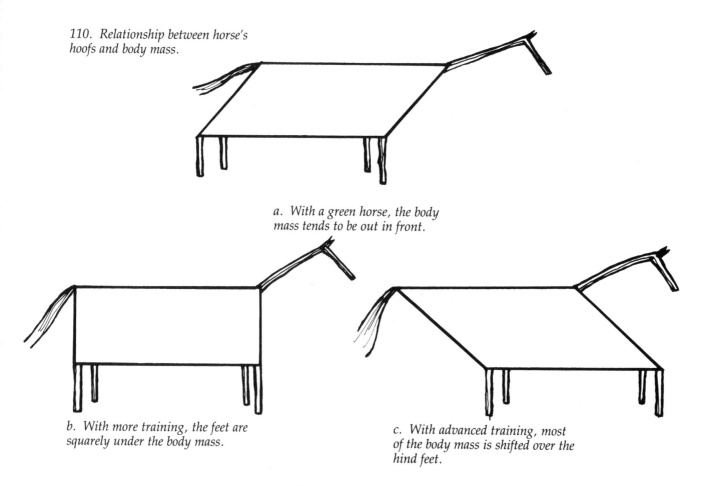

*a. With a green horse, the body mass tends to be out in front.*

*b. With more training, the feet are squarely under the body mass.*

*c. With advanced training, most of the body mass is shifted over the hind feet.*

With a young or untrained horse, all four hoofs tend to be near the back end of the oblong. There is a lot of bulk sticking out in front, unsupported. The front end tends to tip forward and down. The hoofs have difficulty supporting the mass because they have a hard time catching up with the front. The horse's shoulders can't help much because they are trapped by the weight on them, including the weight of the rider. (Fig. 110a.)

With some training, balance in the oblong improves. The horse discovers he can be a rectangle instead of a slanted parallelogram, and can get his hoofs really under him to create a solid, swinging balance. Everything is secure and comfortable, though not necessarily brilliant. (Fig. 110b.)

As the horse progresses through training, he becomes stronger in the rear end and can support more weight with the hind legs. When the rider asks for increased collection, the horse finds himself capable of placing his rear hoofs more toward the middle of the oblong. The hind legs are stronger and more mobile, so the hoofs can support much more of the body mass. This hind-end support relieves the front legs, enabling the horse to do both collected and extended strides. This is now possible because the hind legs can come well underneath before they push off, and because the horse's shoulders and front legs can be reaching, fluid, and elastic. Your horse has, at this point, developed self-carriage. (Fig. 110c.)

When you attain an inner and true balance on a horse, you'll find yourself riding easily with your center over the horse's center of gravity, which lies between the stirrup leathers when they hang straight. You will be balanced over your horse's center of gravity when your stirrup leathers are perpendicular and your feet are under your center. If you can consistently ride this way, you have gained self-carriage yourself, and can then help your horse to attain the same.

A horse without a rider normally has self-carriage— though a stallion approaching a mare has it more brilliantly than the patient school horse. When we put one hundred and fifty pounds of weight, plus or minus, on the horse's back, we make self-carriage more difficult for him. With correct training, however, the horse finds it possible to make the adjustment and to move with brilliance under the added weight. Here a centered rider can truly help a horse.

When the horse has self-carriage, it means that with each stride he reaches the hind leg well under his belly, giving the body increasing support, thus lightening the whole forehand and lending liveliness and gaiety to his appearance and movements. The impulsion is up and forward with buoyancy. As he does this, his neck stretches roundly from the withers through the poll, arching slightly. His jaw softens and his back widens and

*111. Horse with self-carriage. Note the inner balance, the soft, full back, and the graceful curve of the crest from withers to poll.*

lengthens. His legs seem to swing smoothly and freely from his back. He looks happy. (Fig. 111.)

This quality of movement can only be achieved if you give the horse maximum freedom and comfort as he moves. You need your seat, legs, and reins as tools to instruct and help him—literally, to *aid* him.

The constant use of the word "frame" in relation to a horse's self-carriage is confusing, because it suggests a feeling of rigidity. This confusion is compounded because it is possible for a horse to be in a correct frame *and* be rigid, if held there by stiff aids from the rider that restrict fluid movement in the horse. Under a balanced and sensitive rider, the horse will be in the correct frame with no rigidity and will feel almost no constraint. He carries himself and needs only delicate reminders to remain consistent. This is the horse with the correct self-carriage for his ability or level of work. He will be automatically in a correct, fluid frame. He will feel the same sensations within his body as you do when you free your neck, balance your head, and allow your back to be long and wide.

How do you, as a centered rider, actually get your horse to gain self-carriage? It begins, like everything else, at the walk. With your following seat you can teach him the pleasurable sensation of stepping under with his hind legs to create long strides. In doing so he develops the muscles in his back and haunches. He has looser shoulders and learns to handle his whole body under your weight. It is important that you feel at all times the upward pulsation of each step through your seat. As you allow the horse to lift and drop the individual parts of your seat, you are encouraging him to use his back—which is the key to self-carriage. You'll feel that your horse is *in front* of your legs, meaning that he is instantly responsive to your leg aids. If you stop receiving the pulsations of his stride through your buttocks, you will find he is behind your legs.

When you can consistently keep your horse in front of your legs at a walk with the rhythm unbroken, and in self-carriage, you are ready to move on into self-carriage at the trot and canter. Here, too, you must feel the lift and pulsation of each stride—one-two of the trot and one-two-three of the canter—or you will lose the self-carriage and your horse will again be behind your legs. You must remember to keep feeling the upward pulsations of the strides. It requires concentration to do this while at the same time using other aids. If you maintain a really open seat and free head and neck, your horse will respond more readily to your aids, which can consequently be lighter.

Keeping your horse in self-carriage can be helped immensely by your inner videotape. Inside yourself, while invoking the Four Basics, you can see the perfect picture of both of you moving forward together with self-carriage—buoyant and beautiful.

*What are the essentials of the half halt?*
- Understand the half halt as rebalancing.
- Center yourself, then add leg to hand aids as necessary.
- Lighten the hands at the end of each half halt.
- Keep an open, receiving seat.
- Think forward.

*What are the results of the half halt?*
- A deeper, softer, more balanced seat.
- Horse becomes rebalanced.
- Horse's hind legs are more engaged.
- Horse develops self-carriage, which allows him to maintain buoyance without the rider's support.

# 14

## The Canter

In riding the canter, it is essential that you use your following seat with a soft lower back, free hip joints, receptive seat bones and buttocks, and elastic knees and ankles. The motion of the gait is different from either the walk or trot. As mentioned earlier, the walk has a swinging four-beat rhythm and the trot has a quicker, even, two-beat rhythm. In these two gaits, the horse's back remains essentially horizontal. The canter has a longer three-beat rhythm incorporating a pause. The horse's back does not remain horizontal, but tilts up and down like a seesaw. (Fig. 112.) On the left-lead canter, the sequence of footfalls is right hind, left hind and right fore together, and leading left fore; then the horse is in suspension until the right hind comes down again. Your lower body must swing, stretch down, and receive.

112. *The horse's back moves like a seesaw at a canter. Your hip joints must open and close with this motion.*

I think of it this way: When walking your horse during a hack, let's say you come to a dip in the ground that is a few feet down to a lower level. (Fig. 113.) For a moment the horse's back will slant downhill as he reaches into this tiny slide before leveling out again. If you are relaxed, you will simply open your hip joints to drop the front of your thighs down at the same time his back slopes down. By hollowing your lower back very slightly, your shoulders remain upright. Then, as the horse reaches level ground, he brings you back again to the normal position. In cantering you must open and close your hip joints as the horse's back tips down, then up, during the one-two-three beat and suspension. Your hips will be fully open on the third beat of the stride, when his back is in the downmost position. The horse's motion should automatically close your hips at the end of the suspension as his back starts up, which is when his hind feet are reaching under. What you are doing is following the horse's back with your stubby legs.

113. *Riding the three beats of the canter is like walking your horse down a little slide in a cross-country hack.*

*114. One consecutive stride of the canter. Note varying levels of the front and rear of the horse's back, which cause rider's fluid hip joints to open and close.*

The front of your body should feel like a long elastic band. With every stride, it is stretched and released. You must allow your horse to create the opening and shutting of your hip joints while you keep your lower back soft—really let him move you. Ride with your thighs and seat bones wide. Be sure that you feel you are covering the front of the saddle, as well as the part under your seat bones and buttocks, with a wide band of evenly distributed weight. Drop around your horse and let him fill your seat as if it were a soft, well-fitted glove. This relaxed seat will allow your horse to round up under you during the suspension while you remain very deep in the saddle. (Figs. 114.) The front of your thighs should be well dropped, and your knees low and soft, as the hip joints open and close with the flow of the horse. Freely moving hip joints are, in fact, the key to sitting correctly to the canter.

As in the walk, the inside seat bone must be allowed to slide forward once during each stride. It will send the thigh and knee forward with it, producing a slight flexion of the soft knee. Knees that are pinched against the saddle prevent the sliding, making the horse feel resistance, which in turn reduces the roundness of the canter.

There is an undesirable tendency to make the waiting period (during the moment of suspension) too short, to try to start the downward swing too soon. This has the result of shortening the suspension and therefore the stride, causing the horse to lose his rhythm and eventually collapse into a four-beat canter. (A four-beat canter is the result of the diagonal feet landing separately rather than together. This stride produces very little suspension and is not a true gait.) To give the true canter brilliance, cadence, and the proper suspension, you must be patient, leaving your hips open. Allow your horse time to travel through the air. In the canter, the horse does the work for you. Your main job is to let him.

*115. Canter with one hand stretched above your head.*

It usually helps to keep the canter intervals quite short—at first only five to ten strides before a down transition to the trot. There are two reasons to come down to the trot often. First, you may tend to tighten up after the initial few canter strides, and second, the down transition to the trot produces the depth of seat desirable in the canter. You can canter longer periods as it becomes progressively easier to maintain your motion and suppleness. If for any reason you find yourself resisting the motion, just stop and begin again.

As you did with the trot, now try cantering with one hand stretched in the air above your head. (Fig. 115.) Let your lower body drop away and allow your horse to control your motion. With soft eyes, visualize the movement of your body on your inner videotape. If you are cantering correctly, your shoulders will be wide and upright, your head balanced, and your eyes looking straight out. You will feel your heels are back far enough to be under your ears, and your ears back far enough to be over your heels. You will have some of your body ahead of your upper arm.

You will discover that half halts are easier in the canter. Just center and grow with some leg-into-hand aids, if needed, during the three downward beats of one or more strides, and the horse will come under you for rebalancing during the suspension.

Once you are really with your horse in the canter, you will find him enjoying it. He will be happy to canter for long periods of time with you because you will no longer be bouncing on his back or offering resistance to his motion. Remember that in the canter the energy comes up and through you from behind and underneath in a very powerful way and slides away from you repeatedly; forward, out and down in a great circle. As with the walk and trot, it is important, in producing a brilliant canter, that you feel and receive the three-beat pulsation upward through your buttocks. Stiffening of the buttocks and the loss of this sensation will stifle such a canter.

## What are the essentials of riding the canter?
- Use your Four Basics.
- Listen to the rhythm: one, two, three, wait.
- Let your body stretch downhill with the three beats, and wait, during the suspension, for the horse to carry you back up.
- Feel tall, yet deep and soft around your horse, letting your lower back swing.
- Drop your thighs, keep your knees low and feet light in the stirrups.
- Let your hip joints open and close freely.
- Let your inside seat bone, thigh, and knee slide freely.
- Have a following, receiving seat.

## What are the results of riding the canter?
- You will not bounce.
- Horse's back will be free for rounding.
- Horse's period of suspension will increase, improving the quality of his canter.
- Rebalancing through half halts will be easier as his hind legs come under him.

# 15

# Forces of Energy

So far you have been asking the horse to work in a long, low, flowing frame. You've asked for only a little extra energy, and have encouraged him to use his entire body with relaxed, free strides. He has been carrying his head out and down as he gently accepts the bit.

As a rider, you have asked yourself for balance with freedom of joint movement, elasticity of muscles, centered control, and total awareness of the unity of the horse-person. Now let us learn to combine *extra* energy with the flow and rhythm we have already established in our horse-person.

The concept of centering has been well-known in the Far East for more than two thousand years. The Chinese art of t'ai chi ch'uan originated before Chinese history was even recorded. It is the precursor of all the Oriental martial arts, such as jujitsu, karate, and aikido. T'ai chi is a movement sequence based on the martial positions—it is also a dance, an awareness discipline, and much more. In his book *Embrace Tiger, Return to Mountain*, Al Chung-liang Huang says, "T'ai chi does not mean Oriental wisdom or something exotic. It is the wisdom of your own senses, your own body and mind together as one process."

The practice of t'ai chi increases the awareness of your body, yourself, and your connection with the universe around you. You feel the great depth and flow of energy from your center. The Chinese call the center the *tant'ien*. (Fig. 116.)

There are many theories about acquiring energy. Sir Isaac Newton tells us that for every action there is an equal and opposite reaction.

Gravity wants to pull everything to the center of the earth. But because the earth itself is compact, when gravity draws a body down to the ground, the compact ground resists. That resistance is, in fact, a bounce, a force upward, opposite and equal to the downward pull of gravity.

Similar actions and reactions occur in the living body, muscle against muscle, up and down, to keep the parts of the body balanced and upright.

As riders, our problem is that too often we try to provide all the upward activity ourselves instead of allowing our bodies to use the bounce provided by the ground. You can become aware of this upward energy. You cannot hold it in reserve; if you do, you'll lose it. But it is always there for active receiving, so you should use it spontaneously and build on it. Center yourself and become aware of the existence of this energy as you ride.

The horse receives the energy from the ground and transmits it to you through his feet, center, and back. If you allow your own center to feel active, balanced, and in control, you will become aware of the impulses coming from the ground and traveling through you both—upward and outward. When you synchronize this energy with precise aids, the potential for effortless strength and movement grows enormously.

*116. One t'ai chi concept of energy: circles with your center as the hub.*

This energy goes out in a continuous loop recycling through your center. The loops can be small, medium, large, or even enormous; they can include the world or the universe. They can also be any shape, but they will still return to you through your center. This concept of the circular flow of energy can be applied beautifully to your riding; we can build energy deep within ourselves and then transmit it to the horse. The horse, too, builds energy and in turn transmits it to you. The rhythm and depth of movement, and the balance between horse and rider, become easier, more natural and flowing.

When a horse is moving in good balance, his feet can scarcely be heard touching the ground. A horse who is unbalanced and heavy on the forehand, particularly with a stiff or inexperienced rider, will bang and thump on the ground. Anyone can hear them from far away. (Figs. 117a & b.) I once worked with a rather tense rider whose stocky Appaloosa's big, round feet hit the ground so hard that I thought either the animal's feet or the ground would shatter. When he jumped, I was really frightened because of the heavy impact. I didn't see how the horse's bones could stand it. At the time, I was teaching a three-day clinic, emphasizing centered riding, quietness, and energy flow. By the third day, this bulky horse was light on his feet, not only at the walk, trot, and canter, but even over small jumps. He no longer landed with a shattering crash, but with elasticity and lightness. It was very rewarding to see.

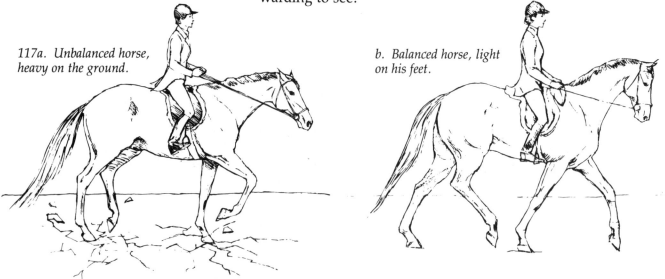

*117a. Unbalanced horse, heavy on the ground.*

*b. Balanced horse, light on his feet.*

The Japanese have a concept known as *ki* (pronounced "key"). It is the extra energy derived from awareness that allows you to do more than muscles alone could possibly do. If you use your muscles to do what *ki* can accomplish, the result would be rough and strenuous, owing to the kind of extreme effort you would have to put out. Using *ki*, you can find energies beyond your measurable muscular output. Your *ki* is in action when you and your horse are moving together with a minimum of effort—resulting in lightness, vigor, correctness, and beauty. Just as the energy and power of all the martial arts come from your center, so does *ki*.

*Ki* can be used in a multitude of ways. Its immense possibilities came alive for me when I was working with a certain student, Marilyn, riding a mare who was a mass of resistances. The mare was a sensitive thoroughbred who had been originally raced and subsequently mishandled. She was afraid of whatever the rider might do. Any down transition was frightening to her. She always expected a bang on her back and a yank on her mouth, so her first instinct when any normal aid was given was to raise her head, increase speed rapidly, and hollow her back. Riding this mare became one long, frustrating fight. So Marilyn and I decided to try using *ki*.

In a down transition, walk to halt, we found that if Marilyn was totally balanced, ear to ankle, supple, and breathing, she could imagine that she was dropping a heavy chain from her center, down through her balanced body and through the horse into the ground. (Fig. 118.) At first, it took the mare six or eight strides, but they were strides without resistance. She then came to a full halt and stood quietly. Soon the down transitions came more quickly. For the very first time, Marilyn managed them without resistance from her horse. We were delirious with excitement.

The next day, she worked the mare alone, using the same techniques. When I returned the following day, we continued to train, and by the end of an hour Marilyn was able to do transitions from walk to trot, walk to halt, and trot to walk. These were done smoothly, with the mare's

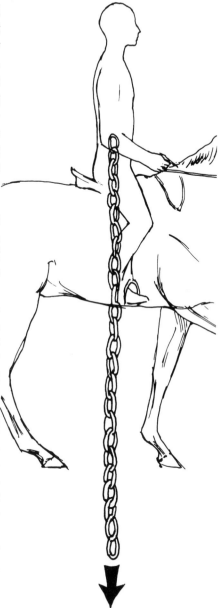

118. Using your ki to stop your horse. Imagine dropping a heavy chain from your center, through your horse, and deep into the ground to anchor him there.

head quietly down, back soft, and strides swinging with no tension. We were even able to go from a slow trot to a somewhat faster trot without going into her habitual mad dash forward. Now, however, with the careful use of *ki*, the buildup of the faster trot could be checked and gradually the slower trot could be regained. The mare's face was lovely to watch, because for the first time we saw her eyes quiet, her ears relaxed and happy.

But if Marilyn was one bit out of balance—if she pushed her stirrups even an inch forward, if she tightened her buttocks or hip joints, if she got excited and put her head forward or clenched her jaw, or (heaven forbid) held her breath—the action was blocked and the mare was not able to respond to Marilyn's intentions at all.

I had another chance to use this technique with Ann, who had a mare that was doing second-level dressage quite well. The mare had one serious problem: She had a tendency to blow up unpredictably. Whenever this occurred, she jumped from the side of the arena into the center and it took at least a quarter of the way around to bring her in hand again. Ann said she had tried everything that she knew of to control these blowups. We discussed the use of *ki* and decided to try it. We had plenty of opportunities for the horse to get upset, because it was an unusually warm midday in February and sections of snow were frequently sliding off the roof of the covered arena. Each time the snow slid, Ann used her *ki* to drop that heavy chain through herself, through her horse, and into the ground. As the minutes passed, the blowups came less and less often. Halfway through the hour-long lesson, the mare was jumping only partway toward the center of the arena; and by the end of the hour, Ann could keep her at the rail, bringing her back to balance, and correct performance, in about half the time that she had previously needed. Though we had not completed the cure in one lesson, Ann was very excited because it was the first method she'd found that had had any success in curbing her mare's explosions.

The use of *ki* is not limited to down transitions on a horse, though it is dramatically effective there. It can be used to take you and your horse over that impossible jump or, combined with the use of breathing, past the most terrifying spook on a trail. It can help you fly in the lengthened stride or go straight down a wobbly line. It can help build energy and balance in your horse for the elevation of the forehand needed in the collected gaits. It is there for use if you have the picture clearly in your mind, eyes, and center—and, of course, have your body balance totally correct.

To develop the use of centralized power-flow and energy, you must develop a meaningful sense of awareness, which involves an inner awareness of your own body and your horse's body. If there are tensions in your mind or body, they will block the awareness. If you hold your breath, you will block the flow of energy. Even a catch of your breath can disrupt the flow. Once you begin to allow your central control to take over, along with breathing and soft eyes, this awareness will develop. You will find that movements that seemed difficult before become infinitely more simple and natural.

You have now received basic training in centered riding and are ready to proceed on a more sophisticated level— namely, your relation to the horse *plus* the central flow of energy between the two of you. This combination will produce smooth power, not rough force.

Let's start building energy in your horse. To do so, you must think again about the relationship between your center and your horse's center. As you begin to build activity in the horse, concentrate on the two centers that coordinate your activity. If you are aware of the critical connection between these focal points, you will soon become a horse-person instead of just a person on a horse.

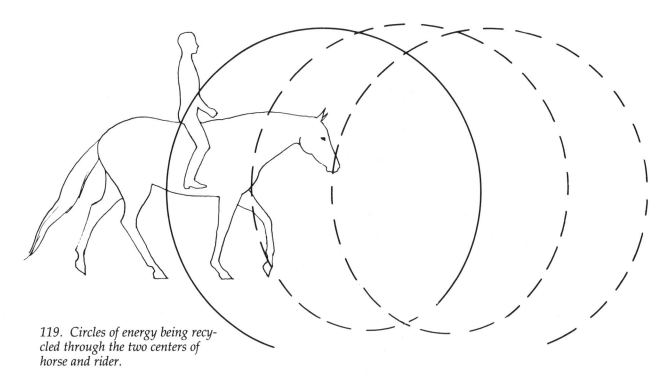

*119. Circles of energy being recycled through the two centers of horse and rider.*

Earlier we discussed the concept of the circular flow of energy. Now you should visualize these energy loops being recycled through the centers of both the horse and rider. (Fig. 119.) They stimulate the horse's back and hind legs, causing him to bring them forward more energetically. As the energy comes up through you at any gait, you can release it out through your arms and down to the bit. Since you want to improve balance and increase power within your horse, you must catch much of that forward energy in your hands and cradle it lightly. Let some energy go through and out, but cradle the rest—just as you would a vigorous, wiggly baby whom you must hold and yet not hurt or pinch. Often energy is blocked at the withers and never gets to the bit. Don't let this happen. It must go totally through your horse; then it will come through again and out beyond. Always retain some of this energy as you build power in your horse. You must keep yourself centered, balanced, and breathing correctly, to allow that energy through.

The horse becomes a well-oiled steam engine moving strongly, pulsating, with all the joints and pistons working fully. His hind legs are the pistons. (Fig. 120.) They come forward and push back again and again, making the flow of energy move up and out through his swinging back. The front legs are freed to swing from lubricated shoulders. The head of steam is controlled lightly and sensitively from your center, the engine's throttle—through your hands to the bit, so that the steam engine doesn't lose all its steam out the front, but instead builds it up within the engine. As this energy builds, your horse becomes rounder, higher in the forehand, and more elegant. The pistons of the hind legs—stifles, hocks, and pasterns—move in a higher, rounder action. You build impulsion in your horse, and your horse comes on the bit. His neck in front of the withers relaxes and the tension of the underside of the neck is gone. The curve of the neck should be the same from withers to poll, not flat in front of the withers. His poll will be the highest part of his body and will be soft. His face will be carried near, but not behind, the vertical. He is light on his forehand and comfortable on the bit.

120. *The horse becomes a well-oiled steam engine moving strongly, pulsating, with all the joints and pistons working fully.*

You have produced a curve of energy within the horse from his hind feet, up through his body, through your seat and hands, and down to the bit. This energy will take the horse forward with increasing speed unless you catch enough of it to keep the same pace. You can do this by catching and cradling it in your hands, letting through enough energy to keep the forward movement you require, and bouncing the unused energy back to be added to the ever-ready head of steam. Think of this as contained energy that can be compared to the popular slinky toy, a flexible spring with coils that bounce back and forth. (Fig. 121.) Every push on one end of the spring ripples through to the other end, to be met by the opposite push that then ripples back again. There is constant activity and bounce between the two ends. This is the activity within your horse contained between your hands and legs.

The concept of bouncing energy is important for the use of diagonal aids in the circle. The energy is like a tennis ball hit diagonally at a backboard. (Fig. 122.) It will bounce off at the same angle from which it was first hit. In the same way, the energy created by your inside leg deflects off the outside rein.

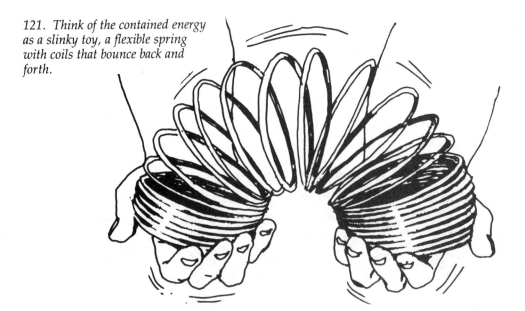

*121. Think of the contained energy as a slinky toy, a flexible spring with coils that bounce back and forth.*

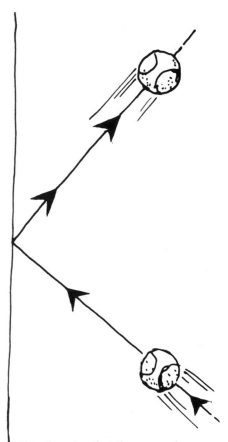

If a horse is correctly on the bit, every aid from behind will flow in a forward curve from his hind pastern to the bit, and every aid from the front will flow from bit to hind pastern. Most of the energy will remain within the horse, always ready for continuous, controlled, springy forward motion. Even at the halt and the rein back, energy must be forward.

If you are to achieve this delicacy of balance in the opposing forces of legs and hands, it is essential that you ride a truly balanced seat and that your Four Basics be firmly established. The building blocks, especially, must be very accurate to allow complete independence in the use of individual aids.

Just how forceful are those opposing forces that we are talking of? Dressage instructor Pam Goodrich uses a telling method to demonstrate this. When she starts to talk about hands, she lightly takes hold of the student's reins close to the bit and asks the student to keep equal contact with her hands on the other end of the reins. Then as Pam talks, she very slowly increases the pressure with her hands—so slowly that the student only unconsciously increases the pressure to meet Pam's. By the end of the talk, the student finds there is quite a hard pull between them. Pam then explains that the horse can become dead and heavy in your hands in the same way if you allow it to happen.

*122. Imagine that the energy from the horse's inside hind foot and your inside leg will bounce against and off the outside rein like a tennis ball against a backboard.*

To meet that opposition, and rebalance a horse that you have permitted to become heavy in your hands, requires very strong leg action or the use of the gymnastic exercises described in Chapter 19. How much better to catch and recatch the energy in your cradling hands, sending it back into the horse's body and your legs for reuse, rewarding your horse after each round with a brief lightening of the reins.

Remember, the conversation between you and your horse must never be dull or inert. It should be, "Ask, receive, give. Ask, receive, give." Ask with your body and legs; receive through your body into your hands; give primarily with the hands, but also with your body and legs, so that you can ask all over again, receive again, and give again. The give is your thanks. If you don't give, you must ask harder the next time, and even harder after that, until you end up with a dead or resistant horse. I have heard Major Hans Wikne, coach of the Swedish dressage team and head of the Swedish National School for Instructors, say so many times, "For everything you ask from your horse, you must give back a little more. The give is more important than the take." Riding is much more than a push-me–pull-you between leg and hand.

*What are the essentials in using forces of energy?*

- Employ your Four Basics, especially soft eyes and centering, to achieve inner awareness.
- Use your central energy.
- Become aware of the flow of energy from your horse's center and its interaction with yours.
- Think of your horse as a steam engine with your hands on the throttle.

*What are the results of using forces of energy?*

- Increased buoyancy and thrust from your horse.
- Greater ease in your horse's carriage.
- Increased suppleness and forward motion.
- Improved brilliance and accuracy of the horse-person.

# 16

## Lengthening Stride

**R**emember how we asked the horse to walk with long and short strides alternately, making him become elastic? Now we shall take this lengthening and shortening exercise into the trot and canter. As you build up energy in the horse, he will engage his hind legs more, and bring his center of gravity back slightly, and shorten his entire frame. As a result, his forehand will lighten, so that when the thrust from the hind legs comes through in the lengthening, his shoulders will be free enough to allow for the longer strides. His frame will actually become slightly longer as he lengthens his stride, shortening again in the down transition. The change will be mostly in his torso, with only a slight extension of the neck.

It is very important that the tempo stay unchanged when you lengthen at any gait. The hoofs do not touch the ground in a quicker beat; what they must do is travel a greater distance in the air between beats. This stretching requires more muscle and balance—therefore, extra energy.

The energy needed for lengthened stride is first generated through the use of frequent half halts to rebalance your horse, as well as many up and down transitions within and between all gaits, including the halt. Include many ten- and twenty-meter circles, serpentines, and lateral work (if you and your horse are familiar with it). Brief canters are also excellent for building energy. All this work produces the needed shorter frame. Keep the program varied. You want to create and maintain interest, as well as energy, in your horse.

You can also use the steam-engine image to build the needed energy (See Fig. 120.) Keeping your speed and rhythm the same, you build up the pounds of steam on the gauge in the hind end of the horse. You control the throttle with small down transitions or half halts as you stoke the boiler in the rear.

*123. Feel that your center is going to fly out between your hands.*

To achieve the actual lengthening, first at the rising trot and later at the sitting, you must let your body grow as you drop your center of gravity, close your legs softly near the girth, and open the front of your body. Feel that your center is going to fly out between your hands, or that your belt buckle is being pulled away from you to where your soft eyes are looking ahead. (Fig. 123.) The horse needs your body to be free and balanced. You can help him by keeping your upper body very upright, leaning neither forward nor back. Just think and *feel* forward.

*124. Lengthened stride at the trot, with energy coming through from behind.*

Your hands must soften so that the horse knows he can go forward, but not so much that his balance is upset. His center of gravity must stay back in his body during the longer strides. He should not be allowed to stretch his neck until after the first two or three strides, and then only a small bit. He needs continuous light, though positive, contact from your two hands so there will be no loss of energy out through the front. That would allow him to drop onto the forehand. The energy must be contained back in his hindquarters to produce the long strides. (Fig. 124.)

After some preparatory work, when your horse is vigorous under you and light in front, you should center and rebalance with a half halt—perhaps several times—then ask for a few strides of lengthening at the rising trot. At first allow only two or three lengthened strides; then ask for the down transition to shorter, but still energetic, strides. A horse needs lots of balance and strength to trot the entire length of the ring with lengthened strides, and you will need much practice to stay with the horse's movement. So keep the number of long strides limited until you know that both you and your horse can stay in perfect balance.

In lengthening, the tendency is to lose buoyancy and energy with each stride. As a result, the horse loses rhythm, and the down transition comes heavily onto the front legs. The subsequent strides in the ordinary trot become unbalanced and awkward. Three good lengthened strides are worth much more than ten that run down and peter out. Before the lengthening deteriorates, ask for the down transition to the ordinary trot.

A common problem is the horse who hurries rather than lengthens his stride. He puts his feet down more often instead of maintaining the rhythm. He does not spring along. This problem is a result of a lack of built-up energy. The horse has not developed that head of steam or coiled the spring in his hind end. Sometimes, too, it's the rider who prevents the horse from moving freely by being behind, tense, out of rhythm, or by giving too much rein.

Here is a wonderful opportunity to apply the circles of energy discussed in Chapter 15. You go into the longer strides, using the rebound of energy coming from the ground. That thrust from below goes through you and your horse, making every stride feel as if it goes way out ahead to where your soft eyes are looking.

Imagine that you feel a gushing wall of water coming through a culvert, pressing against your and your horse's backs. Visualize a warm, powerful wind into which you rest your back, letting it lift you and the horse up and forward. You will fly effortlessly, scarcely touching the ground.

Breathing, as always, is important. I have had students who, after careful preparation, get a surprisingly good

125. *"Horrors! This is no fun. I certainly won't lengthen stride again," says the horse.*

lengthened stride the first time they try. They are amazed at the sensation and ease of it. Their excitement is so great that on the next try they are filled with anticipatory left-brain tensions, and the lengthened movement is much less good, to their disappointment. If this happens to you, don't be discouraged. Take time to think it through. In your excitement, did you hold your breath? Did you raise your center of gravity? Did you tighten your diaphragm or buttocks? The answer is probably "Yes" to all these questions.

Next time, take it as it comes. Prepare your horse as you did before, and during the lengthened stride open yourself to awareness and enjoyment. Play your inner video-tape and let your aids come simultaneously. Let your energy and motion go forward with the horse. So often when we ask the horse to lengthen stride, our centers get left behind. The horse then meets resistance from our hands and body, and says, "Horrors! This is no fun, I certainly won't lengthen my stride again." (Fig. 125.) *You* must be the creative one. You must be the one to project that energy forward with the horse. But remember that your horse must move out in *his* rhythm, not one you impose on him.

I worked with a girl who had a sturdy, capable, long-backed event horse who consistently fell onto his forehand after three strides of lengthening. The buildup for good lengthening was all there, but it was to no avail, until I told her to puff out on every stride. The result was dramatic. She brought him down to a working trot at the end of the arena, her eyes fairly popping out of her head. She had the feeling that the horse could have continued indefinitely in that long stride.

Remember to develop quality before you ask for quantity of strides. If you ask for too much too soon, before your horse's muscles and balance are sufficiently developed, he will start making evasions—such as irregular, uneven, quick steps, and/or heaviness on the forehand. Allowing him to discover these evasions will make it more difficult to develop the pure, lengthened strides, and later the extended strides, that are so beautiful to watch and so exciting to ride.

The down transition is as important as the preparation for lengthened stride. You must prepare your horse for the transition with one or two half halts. The transition then comes through your seat, body, and legs. Don't bring your hands back. The horse must dance up through your open seat into your hands, where he can balance as he changes length of stride. Don't let him lose energy just because it's a down transition; he must move forward into a buoyant, shorter stride.

So far you have been working at the rising trot. The lengthened stride in the sitting trot can be more difficult to ride. This is because the increased motion and thrust throw you out of the saddle. It is important to grow up and down from your center and to emphasize the widening of your seat. With hip joints free, your stubby legs should follow the sides of the saddle downward on each stride. You must also maintain the receptiveness of your buttocks to the pulsations of your horse's back in order to avoid reducing his lengthened stride. Reaching one arm over your head will help you learn the correct feeling. (See Fig. 62.)

The concept and requirements for lengthening stride at the canter are the same as for the trot. Build extra energy and allow your horse to lengthen stride without changing tempo. It is not a mad gallop, but rather a more reaching stride with the hind legs engaged well under your horse's body. Keep your building blocks balanced so as not to throw your horse onto his forehand. Don't lean forward in the galloping position. Allow the horse to fill your seat in the down transition to a working canter, and maintain his forward energy.

## *What are the essentials of lengthening stride?*

- Build the energy through half halts and up and down transitions.
- Use your Four Basics.
- Rebalance your horse with half halts just before lengthening, and again before the down transition.
- Deepen and widen your seat.
- Receive the upward thrusts from your horse's back.
- Go forward with your horse; don't get left behind.
- Keep your hands softly supporting.
- Breathe out in rhythmical puffs with each stride.

## *What are the results of lengthening stride?*

- The horse's strides become longer without an increase in tempo, through powerful thrusts from behind.
- The horse becomes light on his feet.
- The horse becomes more elastic.
- The horse achieves greater engagement of his quarters, and his balance is therefore improved.

# 17

# Lateral Work

In lateral work a horse moves sideways and forward simultaneously in response to the rider's aids. This teaches the horse balance, suppleness, coordination, and increased use of the hindquarters. Good lateral work requires you to be aware of the exact position of the horse's entire body beneath you in relation to the line he is directed to travel. In riding, a horse is *straight* if his body, from poll to tail, follows the line of his travel. On a circle, for instance, a horse is straight if his entire body curves in the same bend as the circle. Such straightness is necessary for all lateral work.

With soft eyes, you will be able to develop the ability to feel whether or not your horse is straight. I like to make very sure riders have this ability before embarking on lateral movements. An easy way to test for this skill is to aim for perfect straightness in the halt on a straight line. How many times, in a transition to halt on the center line of a riding arena, have you felt your horse's quarters sliding off to one side before the halt? Or, if you have successfully kept him straight during the transition to halt, does he make a devastating evasive step to the side with a hind or front foot after the halt? He cannot step sideways without a simultaneous shift in his balance any more than you can step sideways without bringing your body and your center along at the same time. It is up to you, therefore, to feel—through your seat and with soft eyes—that shift of weight within your horse's body before he has time to put out a leg, and then to catch it. You are then controlling his straightness with the necessary correcting aids.

Try to walk your horse down a center line straight as an arrow and come to a full halt two or three times. Feel how he wiggles! It isn't fair! Did you prepare yourself fully with soft eyes, breathing, centering, and a half halt for him? No? Then try it again. Perhaps this halt was better, but how do you perfect it further?

You have already become aware of the problem of slipping the pelvis sideways away from the active leg. It is time now to introduce a more sensitive lateral control for the balance of your torso and seat. Instead of allowing yourself to have only stubby legs, imagine that you have no legs at all, just your torso, which must be kept in perfect balance. If you tip your upper body, you will push your pelvis in the opposite direction and fall off your horse.

Let's start again. Now really go within yourself and balance the torso while allowing your seat to be open, covering the saddle. When you can do circles and halts solidly this way, you will be able to balance your torso equally well in lateral work. Then you can add your legs back on, but imagine that they are attached to your pelvis only with string. Magically, this gives your legs complete mobility for precise aids, but in no way affects the balance of your torso. Your legs' job at this point does not involve helping you stay on your horse. You are now on his back through balance, suppleness, and gravity.

Think of your horse as an oblong table, with you straddling in the middle. (Fig. 126.) It is an unsteady table; the wiggly legs have a way of trying to escape. You control each table leg ahead of you with a hand and each table leg behind you with a leg. You therefore have four individual aids and you never know which one—or which combination of two, three, or four—you may need to use, and when. In addition, when you use one aid it may trigger a response that will call other aids into play. This is where the sensitivity in your seat, along with your soft eyes, is essential.

126. *When you prepare for lateral work, pretend that your horse is a table with wiggly legs trying to escape.*

Remembering that the down transition comes from your two legs at your horse's sides, through your seat, and into your two hands, once again try your straight-line stops. Prepare by playing your inner videotape. Keep using your Four Basics throughout and ride that wiggly table to a steady halt. If you can do this without holding your breath or stiffening and with your torso balanced, you will find straight halts easy and fun instead of difficult and frustrating.

You will find you can sense the start of a shift of the quarters to the left, and by increasing the pressure of your left leg, perhaps taking it farther back for greater control, you can stop that side step before it happens. When your horse stops resisting, you must return the leg to a resting position, but with less pressure, or else your horse will swing the other way. Remember that every time you reposition your leg, you must do it from the hip joint—the old stubby legs trick. The contact of both your legs on your horse's sides must be constant, though it may vary in degree and placement. Precision riding, and this is what you are now beginning to do, is dependent on a constant rapport between you and the horse—using your seat, two hands, and two legs.

When you can use your seat, hands, and legs so deftly and independently that you can make straight halts from the walk or trot almost every time, you will find that you have learned a whole new dimension in the feel and control of your horse's body. Now you are ready to start lateral work.

## *Turn on the Forehand*

The turn on the forehand is a practical way to teach a rider the feel of his horse's quarters and to teach the horse to move his quarters away from the rider's leg. When it is done correctly, the horse's front feet make a small circle in one spot while the hind feet move around them in a larger circle. When the quarters are moving left, the right hind leg must cross in front of the left hind; the reverse is true when moving right. His body, neck, and head should stay straight, not bending around the rider's leg.

To start a turn on the forehand, walk along the side of the arena, going left. Staying parallel to the side, move inward off the track three or four feet. This distance from the rail will give the horse a feeling of not being cramped with his head when you move his quarters around toward the center of the arena. Now halt and prepare to shift your horse's quarters to the left.

Usually a rider's first instinct, when told to make his horse move his quarters to the left, is to use both his right hand and right leg. The horse, having been told to move both ends, does so and pivots on his center, not on his front feet. To move his quarters to the left, the sole aid is from your right leg. The horse's first natural evasion is to walk forward. Your hands must immediately say "No." Having achieved that, they must return to normal contact or your horse will make another evasion by backing up. This in turn may require two legs to bring the horse to think and feel forward again. Now try your right leg again, with all other aids on relax-alert. Your horse's next evasion will probably be to pop out his left shoulder. You control this with the outside, in this case, left rein. Use increased pressure as needed, with the hand lined up with the pommel. The right-hand contact can be very light, but must be there. The left leg must be on, but passive, to give the active right leg something positive to push against.

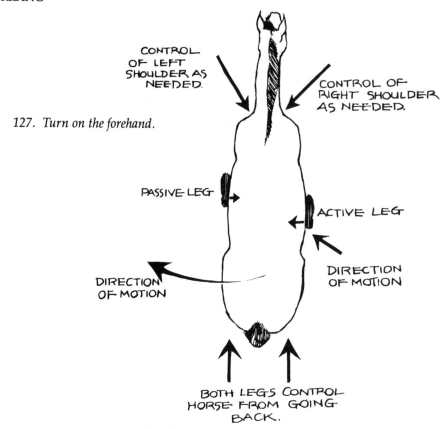

CONTROL OF LEFT SHOULDER AS NEEDED.

CONTROL OF RIGHT SHOULDER AS NEEDED.

*127. Turn on the forehand.*

PASSIVE LEG

ACTIVE LEG

DIRECTION OF MOTION

DIRECTION OF MOTION

BOTH LEGS CONTROL HORSE FROM GOING BACK.

With the use of three aids, you have now blocked your horse from doing anything but moving his quarters to the left, away from your active right leg. With a green horse, it may take some real thumps with the right leg; with a trained horse, only the slightest pressure. (Fig. 127.) When you receive one stride of the hind legs sideways, return all aids to a resting position, stand quietly, and praise your horse (and perhaps yourself, too). Continue, one stride at a time, until you have pivoted 180 degrees, then walk off. When your horse does this willingly, in either direction, try two consecutive strides. Don't let him give you more than you want. When you ask for several consecutive strides, the timing of your leg aids is what he should obey.

For my students, I like to demonstrate this timing while standing. I put my right hand on my right thigh and press it as I cross my right leg over in front of my left. Then I remove my hand as my left leg follows naturally to the left. I then repeat this, pushing my right thigh to move the right leg across again. So it becomes push, ease, push, ease, synchronized with the movement of the crossing right leg. On the horse, you do not remove your leg between pushes, just soften it for easing, and then push again. You will find yourself feeling as if your leg has become part of your horse's leg, helping it to move rhythmically under and across.

You will now find that you can turn on the forehand from a walk, without a full halt. This is a good exercise for maintaining forward energy and engagement of the hindquarters. Remember that in all lateral work, the horse's hind leg that is under your active leg must move across and in front of the other, in the direction that you are moving. If the stride goes behind the other leg, or is so small that it stops beside the other foot, you have lost your forward motion. You absolutely must keep thinking forward as you move sideways. Along with soft eyes, this technique will usually secure the forward motion. If it is still not enough, you must use both legs to make the horse also think forward. You will need to keep centering and rebalancing several times as your horse steps his hind legs around until he faces the opposite direction. Then you must immediately walk straight forward and praise him.

Throughout all this maze of details, your body must remain quiet, upright, and balanced. Perhaps you have been pushing your pelvis to the left and bending your body well to the right, twisted like a corkscrew. Your poor horse! How can he sort out what your legs and hands are telling him with all this unbalanced body interference? The answer is to use all your Four Basics with full concentration and sensitivity.

In learning lateral work, you must keep even weight on your two seat bones. Practice this until you are competent and confident in your skill. Many riders tend to sit on one seat bone harder than the other, but all lateral exercises are excellent for learning the precise use of the seat bones. You must use them evenly before you learn to purposely use them independently. Once you have learned to use your seat bones evenly, you will have control enough to use one more than the other. This will give you an additional and delicate aid.

I once had a student who, when asked to move her horse sideways, leaned well over the active leg, the right leg in this instance, and repeatedly pounded her right seat bone against her horse's back with a sideways thrust to the left. This movement also pushed her pelvis to the left. When I asked her to explain this awkward motion, which her horse firmly resisted, she said, "I lean over and push him away from my seat bone." This method could never work. In order to push something, you must have something opposing to push *from*. Standing beside your horse, you are braced against the ground, but you can't be on him and push him. You would have only air to brace against. However, you can stimulate the horse, and that is what the use of legs, hands, and lower back is all about.

Earlier you learned the value of generously allowing the horse to slide your seat bone forward to keep him moving freely and softly ahead (see pg. 63). Now you can try moving your horse sideways, using your seat bone as well as your leg. In your imagination direct your seat bone diagonally forward toward your horse's spine. Don't rush it, but let your horse do the work and let it slide in his rhythm once for each complete stride. For a turn on the forehand as well as for leg yielding and shoulder in (to be discussed later in this chapter), the inside seat bone, on the same side as the active leg, should do the diagonal sliding. The other seat bone, however, must still carry weight; to remove it would throw your torso out of balance.

Try going down the center line and, with no rein pressure and sitting quietly balanced, experiment with this rhythmical slide. Almost any horse will drift sideways for you with only this delicate aid.

## Leg Yielding

Leg yielding teaches the rider coordination and sensitivity, and the horse obedience and balance. Leg yielding is a movement whereby the horse does not look or bend in the direction in which he is going. The motion is both forward and sideways, but more forward than sideways. It is incorrect if the steps are wider sideways than forward. The side of his body under your active leg should be soft, so that his legs can move freely. (Figs. 128 & 129.) The poll should be soft and bent just enough to allow you to see the edge of the horse's eyebrow and nostril on the side away from the direction in which he is going. The hindquarters should not proceed sideways faster than the forehand, though it is permissible for the forehand to move in a line slightly ahead of the hindquarters.

How do you actually ride this exercise? First, invoke your Four Basics: This is vital in leg-yielding work. You must be very aware of your torso balance and your independent aids—two legs and two hands and your balanced seat bones in the middle. That oblong table, with which you imagined down transitions on the straight line, can now be moved diagonally sideways.

In lateral work the rider's active leg is called the inside leg. This is the leg you are asking the horse to bend around, the side you want soft for the movement and on which you should see the horse's eye. In leg yielding to the right, for instance, your inside leg is on the left. The same is true for your rein.

Your primary aid will be this inside leg. You want the horse's body and rib cage to be soft, though not bent, on the left side. Your active leg must feel long and soft, with no tense joints—hip, knee, or ankle. This primary aid with the help of your diagonally sliding seat bone will urge the horse both forward and sideways. Use your leg in rhythm, as you did when executing the turn on the forehand.

128. *Correct leg yielding to the right.*

129. *Incorrect leg yielding to the right. Horse popping shoulder; rider's legs uneven and stiff.*

You must also use two secondary aids, the outside rein and leg. Since we are leg yielding to the right, the outside rein, the right rein, will control the amount of forward motion; it will also meet the diagonal drive from the inside left leg and seat bone. The outside rein will serve to keep the neck straight and the shoulder from popping out and going sideways faster than the hindquarters. Also, if the forehand gets stuck and doesn't move to the right, the outside (right) rein can act as an opening, leading rein as needed. The outside right leg stays on the horse to meet the push of the active left leg and helps maintain forward motion; it also prevents the hindquarters from swinging too far to the right.

Your fourth aid, the inside hand, is also a secondary aid. It helps the inside leg to soften the horse's side. It asks the horse to bend enough at the poll to give the rider a view of the edge of his inside eye; this is achieved with either a slightly opening rein when the horse is just learning, or a direct rein when the horse has more experience. It must always be a sensitive, forgiving, asking, and generously rewarding hand. Remember that the inside leg must come on before the inside hand when softening the horse's side and asking for the slight bend.

With a horse or rider who is new to leg yielding, I insist first on only small, but very exact, sideways motions. (Fig. 130.) Initially, while walking forward to the right, the horse should move a step or two sideways, in such a way that the left hind foot steps forward a good deal but *across* only enough to come down on a line directly under the horse's centerline, supporting its mass while the right hind moves diagonally forward, completing the stride. The body mass then shifts over; the right foot becomes the supporting foot while the left foot comes ahead of the right again to take on the support of the mass, and so forth. The front feet will make the same pattern. Naturally, if you are moving to the left, all the above lefts and rights are reversed.

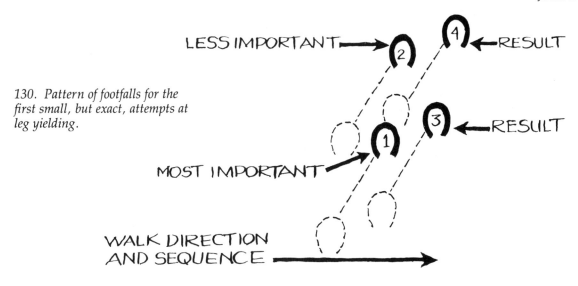

LESS IMPORTANT⟶ ⟵RESULT

⟵RESULT

*130. Pattern of footfalls for the first small, but exact, attempts at leg yielding.*

MOST IMPORTANT

WALK DIRECTION AND SEQUENCE ⟶

This small amount of sideways movement will allow a green, and therefore less strong, horse to stay in balance and keep his back level. A green horse cannot step too far across laterally without tipping his hip down on the reaching side. He tends to drop on the left side, as he reaches his left leg across to move right. Only when he becomes more supple, stronger, and better balanced can he successfully step beyond his median line.

Now practice this exercise yourself. Walk your horse down the center of the ring. Keeping your head and eyes up, center yourself, give your horse a half halt, and, with your left leg behind the girth and your sliding left seat bone, move his left hind foot plus the whole of his body to the right; then soften to thank him for that stride, and ask again. Each thank you to your horse is a momentary softening of your hand, body, and legs. Greater praise includes a pat and frequent use of voice as well.

With your soft eyes, centering, breathing, and inner videotape, keep playing with this precise exercise. Feel that your seat covers the whole saddle, so that your body is stable and balanced and your legs and arms are free to move independently. As you improve, ask for more consecutive steps, remembering to keep your torso balanced. Practice the lateral movement for a few minutes, then move straight forward for a while, coming back to the lateral work again after another few minutes. You can leg yield from anywhere; off a straight line, across the diagonal, or out of the circle on the open side. When your horse responds well at the walk, try it at the trot. You may find this easier than the walk because of the diagonal, two-beat nature of the gait.

When you and your horse are proficient at this small, controlled leg yielding, your horse will have become stronger, more supple, and better balanced. At that point, you can ask him to reach across farther with the inside hind leg. Ask for all the stretch he can give you, short of tipping his back. If he gets upset or unbalanced, return to the little strides you began with; in this way, lateral work remains fun and easy for both of you. The steps must come in a consistent tempo, and the energy, as always, must move from back to front.

If things go wrong, stop and think of your checklist. Were you holding your breath? Was your balance up high, not centered deep down? Did your left brain monopolize and give your right brain no chance to take over? Was your inside leg stiff and uncomfortable for your horse, or your inside hand locked instead of giving? Were your outside aids not on the job so the horse was not contained within them? Or was your horse just not listening? If that's the case, you should remind him that if he doesn't move sideways and forward off your leg, you will use your whip just behind your leg. Remember to reward him when he obeys it. If you, not the horse, were the problem, don't fuss, just take time to reorganize yourself, so that your aids can be precise and clear. Do a few other easy movements and then, trusting yourself and your horse, step sideways again.

## Shoulder-In

Now that you understand the use of aids for lateral movement, you can learn different lateral exercises more easily. Another exercise to develop your coordination and your horse's balance and suppleness is shoulder-in. In this movement the hind legs remain on the track while the shoulders are carried slightly inside. (Fig. 131.) The result is that the horse travels on three tracks: the outside hind leg in one, the inside hind and outside front leg in another, and the inside front leg in the third. The horse bends around the rider's inside leg as he moves forward. He is, therefore, bent away from the direction in which he is moving. Shoulder-in helps to supple the horse and make the hindquarters more active.

A common problem with shoulder-in work is that the rider is so interested in the shoulder and in getting the front feet off the track, that she forgets the hind end. As a result, the horse does not bend and the whole intent of the exercise is lost. (Fig. 132.) Ideally, the shoulder-in is a movement full of self-carriage, with much of the horse's weight carried and balanced over his inside hind leg. The forehand is thus lightened and free to bend.

If you are fishing with a flexible rod and a fish takes your line to the left, you will keep the handle of that rod quietly but firmly headed forward, even though the rest of the rod is bending left. So must you keep the hind end of the horse moving straight forward, held there by your seat and legs. The impulsion to bend must come from behind, with your inside leg and diagonally sliding seat bone creating energy into your outside rein, and with a gently beckoning inside hand for direction. If you pull the forehand off the track with the inside rein, you will cause the horse to take his weight off the hind legs and your shoulder-in will fall apart. So once more you must ride with inner balance and centering, with your soft eyes up and straight out over the track.

131. *Shoulder in to the right, showing correct bend of the horse from tail to poll and the centered balance of rider.*

132. *Shoulder in to the right, showing incorrect positioning, overbending of head and neck.*

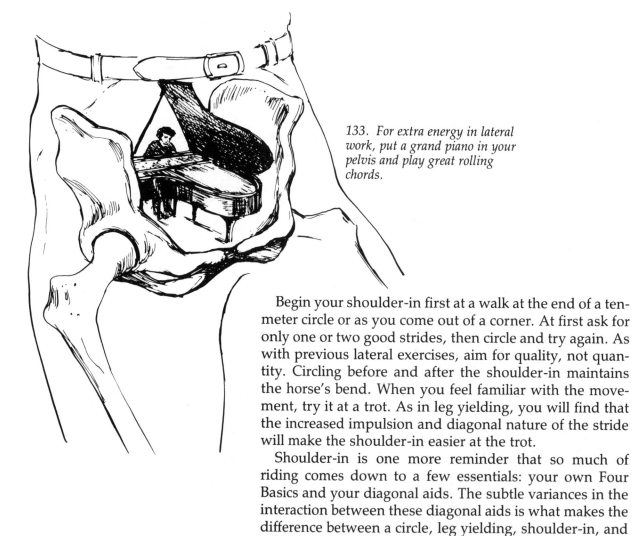

*133. For extra energy in lateral work, put a grand piano in your pelvis and play great rolling chords.*

Begin your shoulder-in first at a walk at the end of a ten-meter circle or as you come out of a corner. At first ask for only one or two good strides, then circle and try again. As with previous lateral exercises, aim for quality, not quantity. Circling before and after the shoulder-in maintains the horse's bend. When you feel familiar with the movement, try it at a trot. As in leg yielding, you will find that the increased impulsion and diagonal nature of the stride will make the shoulder-in easier at the trot.

Shoulder-in is one more reminder that so much of riding comes down to a few essentials: your own Four Basics and your diagonal aids. The subtle variances in the interaction between these diagonal aids is what makes the difference between a circle, leg yielding, shoulder-in, and more advanced lateral movements.

In doing any sort of lateral work, it can help to imagine that you are playing a grand piano that sits in the bottom of your pelvis. (Fig. 133.) A piano is heavy and the image will help you keep your center of gravity down. Play the piano vigorously on the full width of the keys, and let the waves of sound go all through your body. This image will help produce the energy to move sideways instead of totally forward. Lateral work is like playing the piano in still another way: You must learn it piece by piece. You must learn the simple things before you can use each part of your body, like each finger of your hand, easily and without confusion.

Be sure to keep your building blocks one above the other. The usual tendency is to collapse the body on the side of the active leg. It is important that you don't do this, since it throws the horse off balance. When you were practicing full halts on a straight line, you balanced with your torso only, without help from your legs. You must always play an inner videotape of the entire movement before you start, and keep the image in the right brain throughout. Gradually, as you get the coordination and control that you are looking for, you will find that the rhythm of lateral work comes more and more easily. It becomes a dance with energy and lightness—the same whether you are moving forward or laterally.

### What are the essentials of lateral work?

- Use your Four Basics.
- Have an inner awareness of your horse's body and leg position.
- Keep your torso balanced.
- Keep your legs, seat, and hands working independently.
- Always think forward.
- Be precise in positioning the horse for each particular movement.

### What are the results of lateral work?

- Your horse will become more attentive.
- Increased balance and coordination with the movement of the horse.
- Your horse will become more supple and balanced.
- Increased engagement of your horse's hindquarters.

# 18

# Jumping

Just after I taught a flatwork clinic at the University of Kentucky, instructor Karen Winn wrote me, "Your basics work fantastically over jumps! Centering keeps you from jumping ahead of your horse and lets you follow any kind of a jump your horse makes. It also keeps you on if the horse ducks out or refuses. Slow-motion videotaping (right brain), helps the rider from being in a hurry to get to the fence. Soft eyes, breathing, and building blocks, of course, lock right in there, too."

Why is this all so? Principally because the two major building blocks must be one above the other in jumping exactly as in flatwork. (Fig. 134.) In a jumping seat, the pelvis is behind the line of the building blocks, and the head and shoulders are in front, balancing the weight of the pelvis. The center, however, remains directly over the feet, and the stirrup leathers hang perpendicular from the stirrup bars, so that your center is also over the horse's center of gravity.

This positioning means that there is a balance of weight between a series of levers that act as shock absorbers through the action of the ankles, knees, and hip joints. These joints must not be rigid, and should be fluid even when being strong. This allows the motion of the horse to be absorbed and the essential balance of center over feet to be maintained.

Now add to this image the use of soft eyes with the right-brain videotape, centering, and breathing. Your center will stay totally with your horse's center of gravity. You will be tuned into your horse so that you stay with him— not ahead or behind or too high above. Your video allows you to see your total jump, so you don't have to rush to it in a panic. And your centered breathing keeps the whole process fluid.

134. *In a jumping seat, the pelvis is behind the line of the building blocks; the head and shoulders are in front, balancing the weight of the pelvis.*

You will need to have a tighter seat than when you're on the flat because of the increased and, at times, unexpected activity of the horse; but at no point must it be locked, or else you will not be fluid. Shorten your stirrups until they hang slightly above your anklebone. (Fig. 135.) Push your pelvis farther back in the saddle than you did for flatwork. Make sure you keep the stirrup leathers hanging perpendicular from the stirrup bars. This means that your lower legs will feel more upright. Allow your lower legs to press firmly on your horse's sides just behind the girth and your heels to sink well down in your stirrups. You will feel that the bottoms of your feet look forward. Your anchor on the horse is this wedge of pressure between your stirrups and your lower legs on his sides. The weight of your body balances above this secure wedge. Your knees should be close to the saddle but not pinched against it; that would tend to make them rigid, and they must be free to flex throughout the jumping procedure.

Now balance your body over your solidly placed feet by bending forward from your hip joints enough to place your center over the feet but never ahead. The closing of the hip joints is the key to fluid jumping. As they close they will lighten or just barely lift your buttocks and seat bones from the saddle and point them backward. But don't poke them toward the sky. Your jumping seat should be close to the saddle, yet your weight should be on your stirrups and in your lower legs, with that solid hold at the bottom. Your lower legs, thighs, and body create the shock absorbers mentioned earlier. Your ankles, knees, and hips are hinges—the hips the most active hinges and the knees second. That doesn't mean the ankles are rigid, just that they have less room for motion, since the heels remain constantly down but with a springy feel in them.

This jumping position, center over feet, leaves your arms and hands free to move forward as needed. There will be times, on the approach to a jump, that the torso

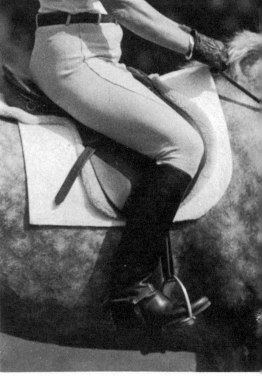

*135. Correct stirrup length and leg position for jumping.*

must be more upright for control and balance of the horse; this may shift your center slightly behind your feet, but as you reach the jump you *allow the horse* to close the angle of your hips, putting your center directly over your feet again for the remainder of the jump.

The tendency for most people learning to jump is to throw the upper body forward while stretching the arms and hands even farther forward. This invariably places the rider's center ahead of his feet and his buttocks in the air, not only making him insecure but throwing his weight ahead of the horse's center of gravity. As in all riding, minimum motion is best and least disturbing to the horse's effort. The closer your center is to your horse and his center of gravity, the more stable and yet flexible you will be.

As you balance in this position over your stirrups, pay attention again to the position of your lower legs and feet. The toes should neither be artificially turned to be parallel to the horse nor allowed to point too far out sideways. The former creates tensions in the knees and hips; the latter pulls the knees away from the saddle. Let the feet be as near parallel to the horse as you can without unnatural effort. Allow the weight of your body to wedge your heels down and press the sides or corners of your lower legs in against the horse. The degree of outward turn of your toes will vary with your conformation and that of the horse.

Try this anchored, balanced seat at the walk and then at the trot and canter. Become familiar with the stable feeling of your feet and lower legs. If your feet drop back, they will be of no help for a quick stop; with the soles of your feet under you and facing forward, the needed brace is there even with the stirrup leathers hanging perpendicular.

With this secure base, maintaining your soft eyes and breathing, the motion of the horse is easily absorbed and followed by the cushioning effect of the shock absorbers. Be aware also of the balance of your center over your feet and of synchronizing this balance with that of your horse. Notice how strong, yet fluid, you have become. Once you establish this basic position in your right brain, you are free to adapt it to varying circumstances.

Now set up trotting rails on the ground, three or four of them, four and one-half feet apart. With your horse walking freely into your hands on soft contact, walk him over the rails until he does so quietly, adjusting his stride to the spaces. Next, try trotting. As you approach the rails, try to see the correct spot from which your horse will step evenly over the first rail in a normal trotting stride. Establish your balance and pace well ahead of the rail and ride him to this spot by maintaining a good rhythmic trot, forward and in balance. This is called "finding your distance" or "seeing your spot." This ability will improve with practice. Think and look forward and straight. Post to the trot and do not plunge your body forward even a little bit. Just let the horse's body come up and down underneath you, your joints absorbing any added motion. Keep centered.

When the trotting rails are easy, and comfortable, set up a small jump about nine feet from the last trotting rail. Use crossed rails about one foot high. Later you can raise them slightly. Ride the trotting rails as before, and after the last one slide your hands out on the horse's crest (the top line of his neck) two or three inches so that there is some slack in the reins. This is called the "crest release." (Fig. 136.)

*136. Jumping through a gymnastic line.*

Leave your hands there, holding a little of your upper body weight on them until after he has made a bigger trot or perhaps a small jump over the crossed rails. Do not plunge your body forward, but notice how, if he makes a little jump, he closes the angle of your hip joints. Let him do that and let the joint open again as you move on.

After you are both comfortable over that jump, add a second one nine feet from the first jump—a single rail two feet high, with a ground line. Ride just the same way, without plunging forward, but maintaining that quiet, secure balance over your feet. Be sure your hands remain on the horse's crest until *after* the second jump, while your hips, knees, and ankles absorb the motion. Then regain your more upright position, using your body to help rebalance your horse. While riding around the ring for your next passage through the rails, establish your balance and forward rhythmic trot, which will allow the horse to come to the right spot and start through the rails without an increase in speed.

When this goes well, add another jump eighteen feet away. Keep adding until you have five or six jumps, each eighteen feet apart. These can be small oxers or single-rail verticals. Always start with small fences, from two feet to two feet six inches in height. You may vary this pattern depending upon the training requirements for the horse. This sort of exercise is standard gymnastics, which can be used to help you learn the feel of the horse's movement over fences, as well as improving his jumping form and balance. In addition, in this sort of gymnastic exercise, the preset distances between jumps eliminate some of the difficulties of getting to the right spot for each individual fence. This simplifies the initial learning experience.

In a jumping series like this, the key factors are quietness with balance, a deep, stable seat, and quiet hands in a continuous crest release. Again, maintaining your centered balance and soft eyes, let the horse do the work, so that he can learn how to deal with his body and legs without your interference. The crest release helps to steady and support your upper body and keep your hands quiet, while giving the horse full freedom of his head and neck. You must approach the line of rails with soft but positive authority. The horse should not slow down or speed up in the approach, but must come in with a balanced, rhythmical, forward stride.

When the basics are learned and firmly established in gymnastic jumping, it is reasonably easy to adapt to the infinite variety of jumps and combinations that you may encounter in any jumping situation—competitions or otherwise. With the gymnastics, you learned a basic seat and a trust in yourself and your horse, and your horse learned to take off from his hocks, to bascule, trust his own ability, and trust you. (To bascule means to arc, like a rainbow, which is what happens to the horse's body as he curves up and over a jump—just as a dolphin curves as it leaps out of the water. The opposite occurs when a deer leaps: Its back is straight or hollow and its head up.) From now on, over individual or oddly spaced jumps, you know how to help your horse in the approach, and afterward to follow him over the fence. Be sure the jumps are under three feet during the learning process, so that any mistakes will not become major catastrophes. Your control throughout must be soft, but powerful. In your approach to the jumps, your torso will be more upright than when you were going over the gymnastic jumps, but be sure to keep your seat light and your weight in your lower legs and stirrups. This allows you to do a number of centered half halts, as needed, securing the essentials to a correct approach: direction, speed, balance, and impulsion. The horse must wait for you in the approach and not increase his speed on his own or take off too soon. Yet he must have forward impulsion, reinforced by the forward energy of your center.

Try to judge your point of takeoff and then look ahead with soft eyes. Wait for, and allow, the horse's body to close your hip joints as he rises, bringing your center near the pommel, where you will quietly remain during the flight. As he closes your hip joints, do the same as before: Slide your hands out a few inches on his crest and leave them there until he has his feet on the ground. The loop in the reins should still be very slight. During the flight keep your seat back and your lower legs and feet forward, just as you did in the gymnastics. Your chief aim after the approach is still to let the horse do the work and not interfere with his effort. You should feel very secure; you are now very aware that your point of balance is close to, and over, the horse's point of balance. (Figs. 137a–c.)

Just as you used centering to help your horse in the approach, you must do the same in the landing and after the fence. Let the horse open the angles of your hips and knees as you come down. Don't flop forward on the landing; you won't if your feet have stayed forward and under you. As your horse takes his first stride on the ground, regain your contact with your hands, but do your steadying with your body before you use your hands. Bring your upper body back, drop your center, breathe, and bring him softly, but firmly if necessary, under you for the next approach to a jump. The more you ride, and control your horse with your body in the approach and landing, the more likely a horse-person will emerge. Use you Four Basics again. Use your body, legs, and hands, in that order. Unify your center and the horse's balance with your feet under you throughout.

137a. Approach.

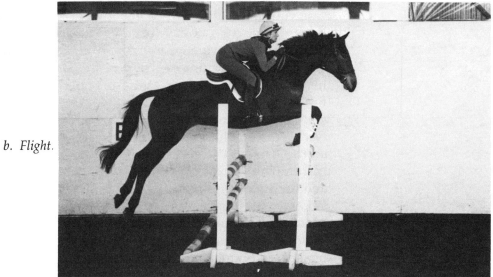

b. Flight.

c. Landing. Note how horse's movement closes and opens rider's hip joints.

You will have difficulties if you block or lock any portion of your motion. First, you will be left behind your horse's motion and then pitched ahead of it, maybe to disaster— like having a nasty fall over the horse's head. In a reflexive attempt to avoid that, you would have to use tremendous leg muscle and maybe even, heaven forbid, rely on the reins to keep you on. In doing so you would prevent the horse from using the total athletic potential of his body over the jump; he would have to compensate for this big *thing* on his back that isn't really unified with him, making jumping not only more difficult but also less fun. He has to make most of the adjustments by flattening his back and raising his head, which in turn flattens his parabola— his arch, or curve—over the jump. This makes it harder for him to snap up his knees and hocks, meaning that he is more likely to hit the fence. He'd much rather feel you balanced and fluid over his center of gravity, over the stirrup bars, so that he can shape his neck and back in the correct curve. The horse wants to stretch his head down, and round and lengthen his back in flight; then, with you still maintaining balance and steadiness, he can bring his head up as his front legs touch the ground, and drop it again as his hind legs come forward to land. His back would then remain up long enough to get his hind legs securely under him for that vital first after-jump stride. In short, if you are off balance in the landing, you can really make it difficult for your horse to rebalance himself.

If, however, you can maintain that centered balance, there are numerous advantages. First, your horse will be more willing to jump because he will have confidence in you; he will know that you will follow his motion, which, from his point of view, will help him maintain the rhythm of the jump and also make your weight seem lighter. You know very well how much easier it is for you to carry a weight balanced over your shoulders, as opposed to something hanging and banging from your belt. Your horse feels the same way.

Second, if you are in good, centered, soft-eyed balance, you will be far more sensitive to any resistances or hesitations your horse may develop. Furthermore, because of this balance, your aids are ready for immediate use. If the horse hesitates, your lower legs are right there for greater push. If he hesitates a lot, it is no effort to bring your shoulders back, with your thighs and knees secure against the front of the saddle. In this position you can drive the horse forward strongly with your back and lower legs, and still be able to drop your pelvis back in the saddle, and the rest of your body down, as the horse comes up to you on the takeoff.

I must stress that breathing is all-important. Countless instructors have discovered the advantages of having their pupils sing while going over jumps—you cannot hold your breath when singing. It isn't just the mental fun and relaxation of singing that makes the jumping go so well; the singing keeps your diaphragm in motion, which in turn keeps the rest of your body fluid instead of locked. So try breathing in rhythm with your horse's strides as you approach. Then, as you take off, let the air start to flow *out*. After that, just breathe normally. The main idea is that if you are breathing out as you take off, it is difficult to catch and hold your breath. If you do hold your breath, you will stiffen, lose your flowing following motion, and consequently be left behind.

What about the rushing or refusing horse? Most horses rush, refuse, or run out because they have had a past experience of being hurt. Some rush because their riders become anxious and override them by hustling or chasing them too much to their fences. If your horse has been overridden, or perhaps frightened because he has been overfaced with jumps too difficult for his level of training, or hurt on a jump, you will have to start out with many low, easy jumps. You must be sure to remain centered, soft-eyed, balanced, and breathing until he gains or regains confidence in himself and you. If, on the other

173

hand, he is a very capable jumper but has been hurt by people jabbing his mouth over fences, or banging down on his back, you have to go the same route, but for a different reason. You have to let him know, through practice, that you will not be left behind his motion, making him uncomfortable and hurting him. You will have to do lots of breathing, because it takes a lot of control *not* to catch your breath when the horse jumps unexpectedly from too far away or too close to the fence. If he does, you should exhale and, leaving your pelvis level on his back, allow your shoulders to swing back, as needed, while you release the reins enough so as to pull on his mouth.

If the horse continues to refuse, it probably means he has been spoiled by poor riding and/or lack of discipline. Horses that are innately lazy or uncooperative are especially prone to being spoiled. You may need to sit deep and use your whip. Be positive, but not brutal. Then, as with a frightened horse, start training with small jumps and give lots of praise for every successful effort.

Now, you may ask, what about those huge Grand Prix jumps? Many of the Grand Prix riders don't have their centers over their feet during the flight. True, but this is the exception to the rule of center over feet. If you scrutinize photographs of some of the great jumpers, notice where the *horse's* center of balance is at the point of the jump that the photograph records. You will find that the rider's *center* is over the horse's center of gravity regardless of where his feet are.

In those jumps that are close to or over six feet in height or width, the horse must execute an enormous snap and thrust. He comes up to the jump with his hind legs way under him, almost sitting on them, and then gives an almost violent thrust up and over, much greater than in smaller jumps. He throws his balance as far forward as the middle of his neck in ascent, and as far back as his loins or hindquarters in descent. The rider simultaneously, in spite of the thrust and snap, must float his center over the horse's balance. It is not always possible for him to keep his feet under his center through these radical changes. Therefore, his feet are allowed to take care of themselves as long as his fluidity is maintained; and his center follows that of the horse. (Fig. 138.) In this way, any interference with his horse's effort and movement is minimized.

*138. Bernie Traurig on Ptarmigan, owner Brumath Stables, Florida 1982 Tampa Grand Prix.*

*139. Bill Steinkraus on Night Hawk at Cologne, Germany.*

International jumper Bill Steinkraus, in Neil French-Blake's book *The World of Show Jumping*, says, "I am considered to be a stylist, but I don't think I consider myself someone who, when jumping, is thinking of style at the expense of the horse. It is important for anyone learning any sport to begin by getting his style right. The foundation must be correct before you begin to build the house. Afterward you can ignore the mechanics and develop in your own way. . . . So I don't reject style—but I am aware that in some people a rigid adherence to it has limited their achievements. The classical ideal can be a millstone around the neck." (Fig. 139.)

Most of the jumping we do with our horses is best done in the classical seat, keeping building blocks balanced with center over feet. This seat will take you through all basic forms of jumping—gymnastic, Medal Maclay, show hunter, and even eventing. All these activities allow a horse to jump from his normal stride in a good parabola, without the extreme upward thrust needed in the Grand Prix classes. If you are jumping with your Four Basics well in mind, you will do your horse little harm even when he makes a mistake.

176

## What are the essential of jumping?

- Keep your center over your feet.
- Use soft eyes and lots of breathing.
- Keep a strong and stable lower leg and foot.
- Wait for the horse and allow him to close and open the angle of your hips.
- Keep your pelvis back.
- Keep your hands forward and soft along the horse's crest.

## What are the results of jumping?

- Centered balance throughout the jump.
- Correct forward impulsion of your horse.
- Minimum interference, even if your horse makes a mistake.
- Jumping with, not ahead, of the horse.
- Security for you.
- Confidence for you and your horse.

# 19

## Suppling the Horse

A supple horse is one who can lengthen and compress his frame as well as bend his body laterally without losing his balance. Major Hans Wikne continually emphasizes in his teaching the necessity of putting the horse through a series of gymnastic exercises in his flatwork. These exercises will not only quietly supple the horse, but will engage the hindquarters increasingly as they build energy, bringing the horse more on the bit and into greater collection. This is all done without force, because by training him through the correct gymnastics, he will increasingly need to *balance himself.*

The result is that when he attains the desired balance, he will be maintaining it by himself, not depending on the rider. You will be very much in the picture, however, in that you are still telling the horse what to do and encouraging him to do it correctly by going with him. You do not offer resistance unless the horse starts to do something wrong. Even then, your resistance or correction can be simply a change of gymnastic exercise, until the horse can carry out the original instructions in balance, moving forward in whatever motion is required.

Strict obedience must be acquired through repeated, appropriate work—accompanied by reward, never harshness and force. You will lead the way using the sensitivity and suppleness of your own body as well as the selection of gymnastics you ask of the horse. A horse trained in this fashion by a capable rider turns from one that is stiff, and going on his forehand, to a more supple, balanced, and happy horse in a remarkably short warm-up session.

What are these suppling exercises? Most of them are very simple, based on circles, turns, up and down transitions, and lateral work. Up and down transitions are far more important than many people realize—as a softener, for balance and obedience, and as a builder of energy. Circles of twenty meters decreasing to ten (with more highly developed horses down to six meters), as well as serpentines, should be included in this series of exercises. Turns on the forehand and leg yielding are excellent for suppling, and as you get further along in your training other lateral work and bending can be used.

The success of this program depends on your ability to choose the exercise that will most benefit your horse at any given moment when working in the arena. You must not dwell on any one movement too long—usually not more than two or three minutes—but slide quickly into a different exercise. The constant change asks the horse to keep readjusting his balance. You must not be too meticulous at this point about perfection in each exercise. You can ask for that only after the horse has been suppled. This should not be a taxing, trying time for a horse—just a time for getting his joints and muscles as well oiled as possible. Most of this work can be done at the walk; the more the better, since it puts less strain on the horse. The rest can be done at the trot, interspersed with short periods at the canter.

Denny Emerson once made a successful change in the warm-up procedure for his great horse, York. York, being an event horse, was apt to be very fit and muscular; but he habitually came out of the barn quite stiff in the body. Denny had to spend at least forty-five minutes of hard trotting work, with circles and turns, to get York supple for more exacting work. Then, remembering the suppling approach used by Major Hans Wikne and noted German trainer Walter Christenson, he started walking for the first fifteen minutes in an intricate pattern of circles, arcs, and changes of direction, constantly introducing moderate leg yielding for one, two, or three strides only. The whole exercise was within a twenty-meter area. I thought of it as Denny and York weaving an intricate embroidery pattern. Denny was careful throughout to keep his own body very balanced and easy. At the end of fifteen minutes of this work at the walk, York's body was soft and supple, and he was happy and attentive. The major part of the warm-up was done without strain or fatigue, leaving York fresh for more interesting work. I cite this example, not as a pattern for all warm-ups (though I find it highly successful with many stiff-bodies horses), but to emphasize the need to pattern your program to the individual horse.

What about a warm-up for the rider? I like to start every lesson with a quiet period at a walk. At the beginning of any ride, you should walk your horse to prepare his body for work. Likewise, you should use this time to prepare your own body for action. Really spend this time on yourself, not on planning what to do with your horse. The horse will only go as well as your body allows him to. So first prepare your body and mind, *then* make your plans and act. Get out your best soft eyes, your best breathing, centering, and building blocks. Retire into your center. Just stay there for a while, becoming conscious of how peaceful it can be. Gradually let the motion of your horse come consciously up through your body until his rhythm and yours blend together.

# 20

# Summary

Now let's put together some of the images and movements I have described to you in this book. Then go out and work your horse. Visualize how you want him to look and how you will carry yourself so that both of you work together most effectively. Keep this picture active in your mind. Center yourself and think of your other basics. Give your horse as much variety as possible. Variety makes work interesting for you both. If you are working in a riding arena, don't stay forever on a twenty-meter circle, just because the first ones didn't work. Correct the problem by switching to other things—make up and down transitions, do some lateral work, come back to your circle, then take it to another location and work it again. If you or your horse do things more easily in one direction than the other, always work the easy way first. This gives you the good image and the good feel, and it gives your horse satisfaction. Then try the harder way. If you are honest with yourself, you will find that the one-sidedness that you feel is in the horse is really more often in you. If you can correct your one-sidedness, his one-sidedness will disappear at the same time.

Feel that you have one skin with your horse, that you are a horse-person connected through your centers. Keep the engine building energy in the horse and let it flow up through your center and out, as you use your aids. The precision of your aids is critical. You can center yourself to your heart's content, but if you give your horse a fuzzy aid, you'll still confuse him. Ask yourself, "Am I centered? Am I visualizing myself and my horse? Am I being precise?"

If you meet resistances, you can now rely on alternative techniques rather than muscle power to work your way out of a problem. When you push and bang with your legs and haul your horse around in an effort to overcome resistance, you will only throw your own body around and upset the horse. But if your body is poised and deep, if your center is below your navel, if your legs are surrounding your horse and are sensitive to all the muscles of his body, as well as to energy coming through, you can almost whisper to the horse with your aids and he will respond generously. Use the right brain most of the time and the left brain occasionally to feed into the right brain; but keep the conversation elastic between soft and hard eyes, right and left brain.

To ride this way you need to have a trained body. That is why we did so much work at the beginning with anatomy and the function and use of each part of the body. If things go wrong—even while you are centering, breathing, and using soft eyes—check to see whether you have stiffened your neck and head. Then travel down through your shoulders, lower back, hips, knees, ankles, and toes—any one of which can upset the applecart. Always start at the top, since the head and neck vitally influence *all below*. See the picture as a whole and be aware of how you feel. That is how you will find the problems that are stopping you from being correct. Throw them away. Remove all tensions. Get that tight part of your body functioning again. Edit your videotape, use your instant replay, and go out and work again.

At one time I had a student named Gary. Gary was not an advanced rider, but he had sound knowledge and was a diligent pupil. One day, as I watched him, he looked tense and angular, his plain little mare wavered on the straight line, and her rhythm was uneven and short. My usual suggestions did not help much. The next day I asked Gary to try a different approach. I asked him to be quiet, not talk out loud, not even use words in his thinking as he rode, but try instead to use only feelings and sensations, to search for the feeling of the body moving under him.

I asked him to imagine how it would feel to make each needed correction, then to feel the actual correction as he made it, and follow that up by sensing whether the correction was successful. I told him he must constantly feel and sense what was right, what was wrong, what was needed. He must stay within himself with soft receiving eyes and seat.

It was wonderful to watch the change as he rode. Gary no longer looked angular, but as if he were one with his horse. And the little mare trotted forward smoothly with rhythm, forming the best circles and serpentines she had ever made. Several people who had been watching were full of praise for the way the mare was now going.

But Gary, when he came in, was utterly confused at our praise. To him it had seemed a totally uneven, awkward ride. His horse had constantly tried to change pace and veer off to one side or the other, so he had to keep correcting her all the time. We talked and explained, until finally he realized that always before he had only concentrated on his own body. This was the first time he had listened to his horse and allowed himself to feel her movements—her wiggles and uneven paces that he had been unaware of previously. Having felt them now, he set to work to correct them and it was the making of these corrections that made the ride feel so jerky and uncomfortable.

Gary's face suddenly cleared. A whole new concept of right-brain riding opened up to him. With this kind of sensitivity he could have the finesse to turn a puttering, twisting horse into one who would move with forward, swinging strides. Out he went again to put it into practice, but this time with shining eyes and open awareness in his expression. He realized that from now on he could ride in a fresh and wonderful way—as if he were part and parcel of his horse.

Gary's experience is a typical result of the centered approach to riding. You, too, will think of riding as a beautiful dance, full of motion, aesthetics, coordination, and flow. If your horse is moving well, his feet will be light on the ground. They will touch the ground as if they were springs. His joints will bend freely and vigorously. Your joints will be equally free—from the top of your head to the soles of your feet. Your dream ride will come true.

# Appendix **I**

### *Riding a Dressage Test*

**W**e all like to show our horse to its best advantage when we perform in a dressage competition. To do so, you need to do your homework. (Figs. 140a & b.) You must thoroughly know the test you will ride and the reasons for each movement in the test. In addition, through practice and familiarity with your horse, you must know what will be the appropriate suppling exercises for warming him up for the test. Be sure you know how long this will take.

*140a. Large dressage arena.*

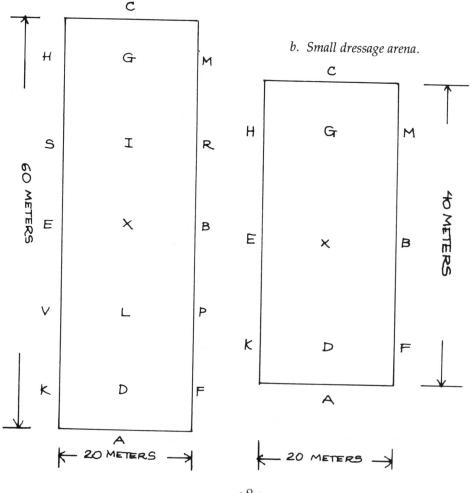

*b. Small dressage arena.*

When you arrive at the showgrounds, allow plenty of time to ride your horse quietly around, so that he can become accustomed to the area and all the activity. Know exactly when you are due to ride. Before you start your warm-up, take five minutes or so to really go within yourself, find your center, establish your soft eyes and breathing, and become aware of the mood of your horse and yourself. When you are ready, begin your warm-up. Ride your suppling exercises as planned. If you maintain your inner awareness, your warm-up should go well, for you will quickly feel any tensions in yourself or your horse and will be better able to correct them.

Plan to finish your warm-up about ten minutes before you are due to ride. This break will give your horse a chance to catch his breath after his workout. It is also a good time for you to review the test. Sit quietly, and with your best soft eyes, mentally rehearse the whole test accurately and beautifully, centering yourself as you do so. In other words, play your inner videotape so that you have a complete performance of every movement in the test absorbed comfortably within yourself, ready for use. You should feel assured that the test will be just one more exercise in your workaday world, and not a terrible seven minutes of trauma.

When the rider before you begins his test, ride your horse again in simple gymnastic figures to reestablish his balance and forward movement. As the other rider salutes the judge and exits the arena, you will be ready to circle the outside of it and familiarize the horse with the potential peril of going between the judge's stand and the arena edge—and possibly past flowerpots. These will not become perils to your horse if you remember to be careful not to hold your breath when going past them. Your regular breathing will give the horse confidence.

When the judge rings the bell for you to enter, go to the entrance gate quietly and without anxiety. After the bell rings, you have a whole minute before you must enter the arena. Take your time, and position your last circle so that you enter through A absolutely straight. Center and re-center yourself as you move through the gate, breathing easily. With soft eyes, look through and above the judge, not concentrating or focusing on him. Ride from your center.

During the halt at X, keep breathing. Feel your legs surrounding the horse, keeping him at attention as you perform the salute. It is important that you keep your building blocks balanced during the salute. A female rider drops her right hand straight down beside her thigh, palm toward the horse's side, making the movement positive, not wishy-washy. She must then drop her head forward from the top of the neck. This gesture of respect for the judge will not disrupt the balance of the building blocks. There is no need for the deep bow that some riders give: This can put the body off balance and upset the horse. A male rider without a chin strap removes his hat with his right hand and drops his arm down at his side with the top of the hat toward the judge. If he is wearing a hat with a chin strap, he salutes in the same way as a female.

When you have finished your salute, quietly take your reins in both hands and have everything adjusted before you start your up transition. Remember to center yourself before the transition. Continue to ride your test, centering and recentering frequently. Remember that you cannot do this too often. Always use your soft eyes, correct breathing, and building blocks. Two or three strides before the transition from one movement to another, center yourself again, preplay the new movement on your inner video, position yourself and your horse, and then start the movement. Use your corners to rebalance and build energy; you should come out of the corners and circles flying, not dying. Consistent, active rhythm throughout your whole test is enormously important. Think forward, above all else, and you will find that the other elements of the ride are easier to achieve.

You end the test as you began it, with a careful and respectful salute to the judge. Then, on a long rein, ride to C, and off down the long side. The quiet, free walk out is important, but there is noting to prevent you from wearing the happy smile you feel inside yourself or from patting your horse to tell him what a dandy job he did even if, by chance, you both had a few not quite perfect moments. They are forgotten. You have ridden a presentable test.

# Appendix II

## *Instructors' Guide to Leg-Lengthening*

Leg-lengthening must be done on both sides, but I will just describe the left. First remind your student to free his neck to let his head go forward and up, and allow his back to grow long and wide. Place your fingers on the rider's back at the bottom of the rib cage. Ask him to imagine that there is a line of pure energy shooting from your fingertips *diagonally* up through his body, out the top of his sternum, and farther up into the sky. He can imagine this as anything that works for him—electricity, shooting arrows, a laser beam, a rocket, etc. When the rider has this feeling, ask him to visualize a second line, which will be roughly at right angles to the first, starting at the top of the sternum and traveling back and up through the nape of the neck into the sky. This will soften the shoulder and balance the head. (See Fig. 51.) These two diagonal forces traveling upward will give the upper body a feeling of lightness. It will also allow the rider to feel his head rise up directly between the two lines. His body should not pull away from your fingertips, but rather begin to feel softer and less ponderous against your fingers.

Ask the rider to maintain the diagonal lines and lightness of the upper body. Touch his sacrum (the part of the spine that goes through the back of the pelvis) to make him conscious of where it is. Then place your fingertips at the bottom of his ribcage and ask him to imagine that just inside his body at this spot, there is a hook from which a string drops to his sacrum. Having understood this, he should further imagine that his sacrum is dropping through the saddle, through the horse, and on down until it is resting gently on the ground. (Fig. 52.)

As this imagery takes effect, you will feel the rider's lower back become longer and softer. He should feel it, too. The muscles of the buttocks and thighs will become relaxed and soft. Make sure your rider is aware of the resulting release. Let him feel his own back with his hand.

If the rider has trouble with this exercise, suggest that he also relax his neck and balance his head, soften behind the lower part of the breastbone, and center himself.

Maybe he should also think about the diagonals again and allow his lower back to lengthen.

Now, you stand with your right shoulder to the horse's left hip and place your right hand around the rider's ankle. (Fig. 53.) Your fingers will lie across the front of the ankle, pointing away from the horse. This hold tends to help the outside of his leg to rotate very slightly forward. Explaining that you will do all the work and the rider must do nothing, ask him to be aware of the position and balance of his upper body, lower back, and pelvis. He should notice that the greater trochanter has rotated slightly forward and will remain that way if he does not interfere with this position. (Figs. 54a & b.) Now draw the whole leg gently back. If the earlier preparation was correct, there should be absolutely no tendency for the buttock to rise off the saddle. The leg will be positioned farther back than the rider will ever need to take it as an aid.

Ask the rider to turn and look at his leg so he will fully realize the capabilities of his body. Also make sure he is conscious of the fact that his seat includes his buttocks, seat bones, and the top of the inside of his thighs near the front of his crotch.

Next, change your position so you face back (your left shoulder to the horse's left side) and place the rider's leg from hip to heel in a good position for an outside aid. Put your right hand around the back of the rider's heel and the fingers of your left hand under the toe of the rider's boot, supporting it lightly. (Fig. 55.) Ask him to feel that his heel is sinking back toward the horse's hind foot with the quality of a stone sinking through water. Have the student realize what a fine outside aid this is, with the buttock and seat bone controlling the horse's back while the lower leg controls the hindquarters. Remind him that an incorrect outside aid raises the seat bone and buttock off the saddle.

An additional factor to note is that when this exercise is done correctly, the release of tension and the resultant position of the pelvis will allow the greater trochanter to hang in a more forward position; and thus the rider's foot will be parallel, or nearly so, to the horse's side.

Next, place the rider's leg in a normal position and put your hands gently around his ankle with occasional light pressure downward. (Fig. 56.) Ask the rider to allow the leg and foot to sink toward the ground. If the rider has difficulty feeling this, you may have to repeat the first instruction of this guide (neck, head, back, diagonals, and sacrum). It will also help to have the rider soften his armpit on this side. When this is done through imagery and not forced action, his leg will perceptibly drop, usually an inch, sometimes almost two inches—much to the rider's surprise. You should point out that this release and drop of his leg, when done repeatedly, can become a valuable inside aid. The drop of his thigh and knee will be felt by the horse's back, and when performed with stirrups, this action will make the lower leg go under and against the horse's side.

One word of advice: Do not pull the rider's leg back against resistance. Your contact is simply to aid in bringing out new sensations and teaching the rider the proper use of gravity. I recall the horror story of an instructor who pulled a rider's leg so vigorously that she was injured for six months. Pulling against tension can cause real damage.

One trouble with leg-lengthening is that when done properly, it feels so wonderful that students want their legs lengthened in every lesson. To help your student be independent of you, teach the student the exercise I call "Being an Indian," which is described in Chapter 6.

# Appendix III

## *Quick Review of Useful Images*

### Soft Eyes
- Keep your eyes open, looking out ahead—not glazed.
- Let your eyes be a tool for awareness.
- Find your center with your soft eyes.
- Let your body feel like jelly.

### Breathing
- Breathe with the bellows in your belly; don't inflate a balloon in your chest.
- Breathe through a flexible tube right down through your body.
- Breathe into your arms and feet and out the top of your head.
- Breathe all the way down to your center.
- Let your whole body breathe.

### Centering
- Think of your center as filling your lower body behind and below your navel.
- Drop your consciousness down within yourself.
- Breathe all the way down to your center.
- Pretend you are a doll weighted at the bottom.
- Look with your eyes from your center.
- Let awareness come from your center.
- The gears for all motion are in your center.
- Energy recycles through your center.
- Power emanates from your center.
- Your *ki,* your life energy, radiates from your center.

### Building Blocks
- Your body is a carefully balanced stack of children's building blocks.
- There is a plumb line hanging from your ear to your shoulder, hip, and ankle (looking from the side). It goes through your center.
- Your center balances over your feet.
- To help balance the building blocks, imagine a coiled spring pulling you up and forward from your center.

### Learning and the Brain
- The two sides of your brain are like water and oil in a moving glass ball, molding with and complementing each other, but not mixing.
- When the left brain learns the feel of a motion, the sensations then pass into the right brain.
- You can trust the right brain to take over.
- Like a child at play, lose yourself from within, during any activity.
- Let your attention touch on the details of your activity frequently, but briefly.
- Play an inner videotape of each movement before you ride it.

### Anatomy
- Ride your bones.
- Your legs hang from your hip joints like old gates hanging from only the top hinges.
- Your legs can move in your hip joints like protruding flippers.

- Imagine pulling the strings on your ankles.
- Tie string to your greater trochanters; pull them out sideways and forward.
- Pretend you have no lower legs but only a weight hanging on a string from each knee.
- Your shoulders are like a yoke, and your arms are the ropes hanging down from the ends, holding pails of water.
- Your head is balanced like a billiard ball on a cue stick.

## Balance and Body Freedom

- To sit evenly, siphon weight from one leg to the other.
- Spread out your toes in your boots to help evenness.
- Ride with no legs, only a torso.
- Feel the two diagonal streams of energy making your upper body light.
- Free the neck to let your head balance forward and up, and your back become long and wide.
- Drop your sacrum on a string to the ground.
- Remember the leg-lengthening exercise.
- Pretend you are the Indian in the statue *Appeal to the Great Spririt*.

## Walk and the Following Seat

- Receive the upward pulsations through your buttocks.
- Pretend you have only stubby legs cut off just above the knees.
- Ride with a wide band of weight on your horse's back.
- Imagine you share a common skin with your horse.
- Be a spruce tree; grow up and down.
- Point and grow one arm up to the sky and let your body drop away.
- Let the wet sand in your upper body dry out and run down through you and all over the back of your horse.
- Let the horse slide your receiving seat bone.

## Rising (Posting) Trot

- Let the ice cream in your body melt down all over the horse and onto the ground.
- The angles of knees and elbows open and shut equally as you post.
- Siphon weight from one leg to the other to keep your weight even in the stirrups.
- Spread your toes out inside your boots.
- Ride with your feet in the mud.
- Think of a coiled spring pulling you up and forward from your belt buckle.
- Ride your horse, standing in the stirrups, with your pelvis in front of the pommel and arms outspread.
- Ride within the parallelograms.
- Stretch one arm over your head with your fingers growing to the sky.
- Inside your boots, spread out your toes and let them play the piano.
- Pretend you are a doll weighted at the bottom.
- Pull the string on your forehead and let your floppy rag body drag through the water.
- Let the buttons on your imaginary shirt come undone to let the front of your body come through.

## Hands

- Your hands belong to the horse.
- Hold your reins as if they were little birds; don't crush them or knock their heads together, but don't let them fly away.
- Hold your reins as if they were partially squeezed sponges.
- Your ring finger talks to the horse first.
- Your forearms and reins form a straight line to the horse's mouth.

## Transitions

- Ride with the interchangeable trio of centering, rebalancing, and half halt.
- Be a spruce tree; center and grow.
- Ride with your stubby legs.
- Breathe out through the bellows.
- Play your inner videotape.
- Feel the horse's body lift and fill your open seat.
- Pretend you are a doll weighted at the bottom.

## Down Transitions

- The front of your body is a long elastic band.
- Drop your stubby legs down the sides of your horse like a clothespin on a line.
- Instead of knees, pretend you have only string connecting your upper and lower legs.
- Your lower legs draw the horse's hind feet under your seat by elastic bands.
- Drop your *ki* to anchor your horse.

## Up Transitions

- Churn up the energy in your center.
- Shoot the beams of energy forward from your center.
- Blow your horse forward with puffs of breath.

## Sitting Trot

- Ride as if you were skiing down a slope of moguls.
- Ride as if you were a car on a bumpy road, with the wheels absorbing the bounce while the rest of the car is stable.
- Fall downhill with your following stubby legs.
- Your lower back is a strong rubber column.
- Be a spruce tree; center and grow.
- Ride with stubby legs and well-oiled hip joints.

- Stretch your hand over your head, grow your fingers to the sky, and let your body hang down.
- Pretend you are a doll weighted at the bottom.
- Imagine you are a puppet hung from a string attached to the top of your head.
- Let the wet sand in your upper body dry out and run down through you and all over the horse.
- Receive the pulsations from your horse's back.
- Your buttocks are a sponge-rubber cushion.
- Ride within your parallelograms.
- Ride your bones.
- Play your inner videotape.

## Circles and Turns

- The horse's body is a bow.
- Feel the sides of your horse with your stubby legs.
- Imagine the bones of the stubby leg and greater trochanter moving through the muscle, as the outside leg moves back.
- Turn the swivel from the soles of your feet to the top of your head.
- Spin the barbershop pole upward before and during a turn.
- There are eyes in the top of your chest.
- The yardarm of the mast, your collarbones, must remain horizontal, not tipped.
- Energy pours from behind like rushing water through a funnel; keep the rushing water from leaking out through the side of the funnel.
- Instead of knees, pretend you have only string connecting your upper and lower legs.
- Your inside leg is not an iron bar.
- Breathe into the inside floating ribs.
- Breathe and center into the right side to turn

right, into the left side to turn left.

- Your outside leg drops to the horse's outside hind foot.
- Your inside leg drops into the ground.
- Play your inner videotape.
- The horse slides your inside seat bone forward.

## Half Halts and Self-Carriage

- Centering causes rebalancing; rebalancing is a half halt.
- Centering, half halts, and down transitions intertwine.
- Your center lies over the horse's center of gravity.
- Be a spruce tree; center and grow.
- Ride with stubby legs.
- Tie imaginary strings to your greater trochanters and pull them out sideways and forward to help open your seat.
- Catch the energy as if you were cradling a baby in your hands.
- Feel the pulsations come up into your seat.
- Your seat feels like a soft glove; your horse fills it.
- The horse's hoofs come farther under the body mass.

## The Canter

- Ride the canter as if you were riding a seesaw.
- Feel as if you were riding your horse down a little hill and back up again.
- Reach for the sky throughout your upper body as you slide down the imaginary hill.
- The front of your body is an elastic band.
- Heels under ears; ears over heels.
- Let your inside seat bone and knee slide forward each stride.

- Wait during the suspension.
- Tie strings to your greater trochanters and pull them out sideways and forward to help open your seat.
- Keep your stubby legs heavy.
- Let the buttons on your imaginary shirt come undone to let the front of your body through.

## Forces of Energy

- Energy can go in all directions—up and down, forward and back.
- Energy gives you power and lightness.
- Become aware of energy through a breathing body without tensions.
- Energy bounces from the ground.
- Circles of energy come from, and recycle through, the centers of you and your horse.
- Catch the energy as if you were cradling a baby.
- Your horse moves forward like a well-oiled steam engine; contain the energy with the throttle.
- Energy bounces within the horse like the coils of a slinky toy.
- Ask, receive, give.
- In a turn, the energy bounces from behind against the outside rein, like a tennis ball bouncing against a backboard at an angle.
- The hind legs swing all the way up under you.
- Feel that more of the horse is in front of you than behind.

## Lengthening Stride

- Be a spruce tree; center and grow.
- Imagine that you are a puppet hanging from a string attached to the top of your head.
- Spread your toes out inside your boots.
- Open your well-oiled hip joints.

- Feel that more of the horse is in front of you than behind.
- Build a head of steam and control the throttle.
- Coil the energy spring.
- Your horse becomes an elastic band with long and short strides.
- Use the bounce of energy from the ground.
- Churn up energy in your center.
- Shoot beams of energy forward from your center out through your hands.
- Your belt buckle is tugged forward between your hands.
- The power of water gushing through a culvert, or a warm wind at your back, push you and your horse forward.
- Blow your horse forward with puffs of breath.
- Cradle the energy in front as it thrusts from behind.
- Fly with your horse.
- The horse comes up and under you in the down transition.

## Lateral Work

- Your horse is a table with four wiggly legs to control.
- Catch the shift of weight before the evasion begins.
- Be a spruce tree; center and grow.
- Ride without legs; be a torso only.
- Ride with stubby legs.
- Your inside leg is not an iron bar.
- Your inside leg becomes a part of your horse's inside leg.

- Ride with the interchangeable trio: half halt, centering, and down transition.
- Play your inner videotape.
- Cover the whole saddle with your seat.
- Direct your seat bone to slide diagonally forward toward the direction of movement. Let the horse do the sliding.
- Surround your horse with your aids.
- Energy bounces from behind like a tennis ball bouncing off a backboard at an angle.
- Play great chords on the grand piano in your pelvis.
- In a shoulder in, hold the horse as if he were a fishing pole with a fish pulling the line to the inside.
- Feel that you are dancing.

## Jumping

- You have only two building blocks, your center over your feet.
- Your center stays over the horse's balance point.
- Keep your soft eyes, centering and breathing.
- Your lower legs in the stirrups, against the horse's sides, form a wedge.
- Your knees are soft.
- The levers and shock absorbers of your hips, knees, and ankles absorb the motion.
- Your center comes close to your horse.
- Play your inner videotape.
- The horse closes and opens the angle of your well-oiled hips.

# Index